REAL HEROES
Amazing Stories From the Bible

Merlin L. Neff

Pacific Press®
Publishing Association

Nampa, Idaho | Oshawa, Ontario, Canada
www.pacificpress.com

Cover Design by Gerald Lee Monks
Cover Illustration by Clyde Provonsha
Inside Design by Steve Lanto

Inside Illustrations
Robert Ayers—pages 8, 9, 24, 54, 56, 59, 71, 80, 87
Joe Maniscalco—pages 20, 23, 27, 30, 32, 35, 38, 41, 47, 51, 56, 68, 79, 92
Clyde Provonsha—pages 1, 4, 5, 7, 10, 12, 14, 15, 16, 65, 73, 88, 89
John Steel—pages 18, 33, 43, 61, 63, 74, 85, 96

All Scriptures quoted are from The New King James Version, copyright © 1979,
1980, 1982, Thomas Nelson, Inc.

ISBN 978-0-8163-2281-7

May 2016

CONTENTS

Chapter 1

God Makes a World

Genesis 1; 2

Let's say that we see a sturdy, wide-spreading oak tree in a meadow. It has stood through storms and winds for almost a hundred years. But how did it begin? Where did it come from?

You spot a tiny acorn under the tree and find that it holds the secret of the oak. The brown acorn, cold and hard, almost like a rock, has fallen to the ground. The sunshine and rain work on the acorn, and soon the life hidden within its shell sends out shoots that eventually grow into another strong oak tree.

Life is a strange mystery. How is life hidden in the acorn? Where did life come from in the first place?

Let's go back to the time when there was no life on this earth. We will start at the beginning of our world. "In the beginning God created the heavens and the earth. The earth was without form, and void; and darkness was on the face of the deep. And the Spirit of God was hovering over the face of the waters." Yes, our earth was a dark planet covered with water; there was no land and no plants or animals. No life, no moving creatures, no sound, no light!

Then the wise, loving God in heaven began to make the world into a beautiful home in which people and animals could live. As He thought about the world in darkness, He commanded, "Let there be light!" When He spoke, rays of light broke through the blackness; light shone upon the water-covered earth. This was the first morning of the world's history. God saw the light and called it Day, and the darkness He called Night.

On the second day God spoke again, and the water on the earth was separated from the water above the earth. The clear blue dome of the sky appeared, and God called it the heavens. We know that the sky is filled with air, called the atmosphere, that reaches above the earth's surface for miles, and that the water in the atmosphere is carried in clouds that you see floating in the air.

On the third day God said, "Let the waters under the heavens be gathered together into one place, and let the dry land appear." Then the waters on the earth rolled and tumbled together to become oceans; and dry land rose up above the seas for the first time. The hills stood out tall and majestic, and the valleys and plains were spread over the earth; but the hills and plains were not yet beautiful, because they were just dirt.

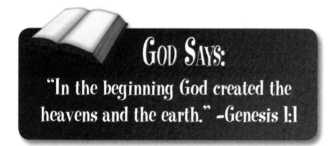

GOD SAYS:

"In the beginning God created the heavens and the earth." –Genesis 1:1

But God continued His work and said, "Let the earth bring forth grass, the herb that yields seed, and the fruit tree that yields fruit according to its kind, whose seed is in itself, on the earth." And it happened that way; the trees, grasses, and plants appeared on the fresh soil that only the day before had been covered with water.

As God looked at the new world carpeted with green grass and adorned with flowers of every color, as He saw the beautiful trees loaded with fruit, He said that it was all very good!

Trees, grass, and flowers grow best in the sunlight. On the fourth day God caused the sun to appear. Its warm rays shone on the hills and glistened on the rivers flowing through the valleys. In the evening, after the sun had set, the moon and stars appeared. God commanded the sun and moon to give light and also to separate day from night. He said, "Let them be for signs and seasons, and for days and years."

On the fifth day God created the fish that live in the seas and rivers; He also made the birds and insects that fly in

QUICK FACT:

God created everything in just the right order. He made sure there was air to breathe and grass to eat before He created any cows or horses.

the air. The new world suddenly came to life with the flash of wings. The fish jumped in the rivers, while bees buzzed and crickets chirped among the flowers and grass. Great whales glided through the sea and spouted when they came to the surface for air. Bluebirds, orioles, parrots, eagles, ducks, pigeons, ostriches—birds of every color and size appeared. Songbirds made the air ring with sweet sounds—earth's first music. Once more, at the close of the fifth day, God looked on His work and saw that it was good.

On the sixth day God made the land animals and reptiles. Think of the many creatures that roamed the earth that day for the first time! The forests and fields were suddenly alive with elephants, lions, horses, cows, monkeys, kangaroos, moose, and a thousand other animals!

The earth, covered with many kinds of grass, magnificent trees, and beautiful flowers, was now filled with the songs of birds and the sounds of the animals. The deer leaped through the grass. The bears climbed up into the trees. The lions roamed about the grasslands. But the animals were not wild or savage as they are today but were gentle and unafraid. Above them was the blue sky and warm sunlight—signs of God's love. But still something was lacking. There were no people to enjoy this perfect home.

God said, "Let Us make man in Our image, according to Our likeness." From the dust of the earth He formed a body in the shape of a man. It was made in the likeness of God Himself. Then the Creator breathed into the clay body the breath of life, and there it was: a living human being! He had a perfect head with eyes to see, ears to hear, and a mouth to speak. He had strong arms to carry things and sturdy legs to walk and run wherever he wanted to go. This was truly a wonderful being, made to look like God Himself!

This man, Adam, was strong and healthy. He could think and speak; he could run; he could swim in the river; he could work. He loved his Creator and listened to all of His instructions.

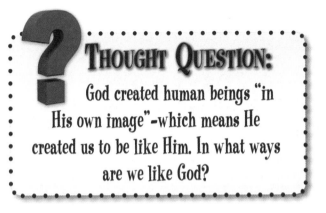

THOUGHT QUESTION: God created human beings "in His own image"-which means He created us to be like Him. In what ways are we like God?

Adam watched each animal. He saw the elephant swing its trunk and look at him with sharp little eyes. The deer was curious and came close to the man. God had all the animals walk past Adam, and he gave names to every one of them. Would you like to have named all the birds and animals? Adam had to think of many names, each of them fit for the creature.

Adam saw that all of the living creatures were in pairs. Not one of them was alone. He began to feel lonely. Was there no one on the earth who could be his companion?

GOD SAYS:

"Then God blessed the seventh day and sanctified it, because in it He rested from all His work which God had created and made." –Genesis 2:3

So God caused Adam to fall into a deep sleep. Then He opened the man's side and took out one of his ribs. God formed the rib into another beautiful creature—a woman. Here is a wonderful lesson for us. The woman who becomes the wife of a man stands beside him as his equal. She is not above him and not below him. She is to love her husband and be his faithful companion in life.

God brought the woman to the man, and he loved her and she became his wife. And Adam gave her the name Eve because she was the mother of all human beings.

At the close of the sixth day God looked over the earth filled with living creatures, which were to be ruled by the man and the woman, and He saw that everything He had made was very good. The task of creating the world was finished in only six days! God's crowning work was people, who were formed in the image of their Creator.

On the seventh day God rested from His work. He made the seventh day of the week a special occasion in honor of the new world He had created. God blessed the seventh day and set it apart from the other six days of the week as a time for people to rest and to remember the One who made the world and created them. We remember the Sabbath too, because it's the special day of the week when we worship and honor our Creator and thank Him for our beautiful world.

Chapter 2

A FLOOD DESTROYS THE EARTH

Genesis 6–8

As the years passed, more and more people lived on the earth. But they became so wrapped up in their business and pleasure that they forgot God and did not thank Him for food, shelter, and all the good things they had. They thought only of themselves and of eating, drinking, and having a good time. They began to kill and steal and lie to get the things they wanted.

Finally they became so evil that God, who loved His people, said He was sorry He had created them at all. It was a terrible thing for God's people, who had been made in the image of God Himself, to fall so low in sin!

A few people were loyal to God and obeyed His commandments. Among them was Enoch, who was the seventh generation from Adam. He probably heard the story of the Garden of Eden directly from Adam.

When the Lord saw that the wickedness of sinful people was becoming worse and worse, He said, "I will destroy man whom I have created from the face of the earth, both man and beast, creeping thing and birds of the air, for I am sorry that I have made them." But then He thought of Noah, who was Enoch's great-grandson. Noah loved God and obeyed Him. He had a wife and three sons, Shem, Ham, and Japheth.

God told faithful Noah that the earth was going to be destroyed, but that he and his family would be saved. Noah was to build an ark, which means a giant boat. God said that a mighty flood of water would destroy every living creature on the earth.

Noah believed what God said and began to build the ark. It was about six hundred feet long, one hundred feet wide, and sixty feet high. It had three decks, and it was made of strong wood covered with black pitch, or tar, inside and out, so that it would not leak.

Many people who lived near Noah watched the shipbuilders working. *What is Noah making?* they wondered.

Noah told them he was building an ark, as God had commanded. He told them that the earth was to be destroyed by a flood of water. Furthermore, Noah invited his friends to help build the boat and to come on board when it was ready. There would be room for them if they would accept God's invitation to be saved.

But the neighbors laughed at Noah and said he was foolish. They had never seen rain, because until that time the earth had always been watered by a mist that came up out of the ground.

Noah was not discouraged, because he trusted in God. When the ark was finished, the Lord told Noah to gather food and supplies for his family and for all the animals. Once more Noah invited his neighbors to come into the ark with him, but they all refused.

Then God told Noah, "Come into the ark, you and all your household, because I have seen that you are righteous before Me in this generation." The crowd laughed as the eight people—Noah, his wife, their three sons, and their wives—walked up the gangplank and entered the ark.

Then a strange thing happened. Out of the forests and down from the hills, animals and birds came. Camels and tigers, bears and elk, lions and giraffes, rabbits and wolves, small animals and large moved toward the ark; and yet no man was herding them. With a flutter of wings, flocks of birds darkened the sky. They flew toward the huge boat and found shelter in it. Two of every kind of bird and animal—male and female—came at God's call. Seven pairs of the animals that are clean to eat, such as sheep and cows, also found safety in the ark. Noah and his family would need them for food after the Flood.

The people who had laughed at Noah looked on with amazement. Perhaps some of them began to worry a little bit, wondering if Noah could be right. But no one decided to join Noah and his family in the ark.

When all the animals were safely inside, God Himself shut the giant door. The rain did not begin immediately. For seven days the sun continued to shine. The people outside laughed at Noah and his family, who were shut up in the ark.

On the eighth day, dark clouds gathered in the sky, lightning flashed, and the storm broke in terrible fury. Water burst out of the ground in huge torrents and began to fill the valleys.

GOD SAYS:

"Then the Lord saw that the wickedness of man was great in the earth, and that every intent of the thoughts of his heart was only evil continually." –Genesis 6:5

Wind drove the rain in great sheets over the land. Day and night the water continued to pour from the sky and from under the ground, and the rivers and seas rose higher and higher. Some of the wicked people remembered

13

Noah's ark. They pounded on the door and shouted "Let us in!" But it couldn't be opened. They were too late!

Forty days and nights it rained. The rising water lifted the ark, and the waves rocked it back and forth. The water rose higher and higher until the trees, rocks, and hills were covered. Men and women climbed the tallest mountains, but they could not find a way to escape the rising waters. The Flood covered all of the land and was at least twenty feet deep above the highest mountain. Every human be-ing and all the ani-mals were destroyed except those that were safe in the ark.

During the storm, Noah and his family were safe in the boat, although it was pushed to and fro by the flood-waters. They must have longed for the wind and rain to stop, because the ark tossed and pitched on the stormy seas for five months! Finally the rain slowed and stopped, but the sturdy craft continued to float for several weeks.

Finally, Noah decided to send out a raven. If there was dry land nearby, it would find a place to live. The bird flew back and forth but returned to the boat, and Noah knew that water still covered the earth.

A week later he released a dove, but she also returned. Noah and his family must have wondered if the water would always cover the earth. But they believed God's promise to save them. Another week passed, and Noah sent out the dove again. In the evening she returned with the olive leaf in her beak. Noah's family was very happy, because now they knew dry land had appeared and they could soon leave the ark.

A strong wind blew and began to dry the flood waters, and the mountains appeared once more. The water dropped lower and lower until the boat finally settled on Mount Ararat. How happy Noah's family was to feel something solid under their feet again!

"Go out of the ark, you and your wife, and your sons and your sons' wives with you," God said to Noah. "Bring out with you every living thing of all flesh that is with you: birds and cattle and every creeping

> **QUICK FACT:**
> There was more floor space in the ark than in twenty-one basketball courts.

15

thing that creeps on the earth, so that they may abound on the earth, and be fruitful and multiply on the earth."

Eight happy people left the boat that had been their home for many months. The first thing Noah did was to build an altar and offer a sacrifice to God for His love and His protection.

Later, when dark clouds gathered and rain fell on the earth, Noah and his sons must have wondered if there would be another flood, because they had not seen rainy weather before the Flood. So God promised Noah that He would never again destroy the world by water. As the sun shone through a shower of rain, Shem and Ham pointed to a great arch of many colors in the heavens above them. "What can that be?" they asked.

It was a rainbow. God said, "I set My rainbow in the cloud, and it shall be for the sign of the covenant between Me and the earth." The rainbow is a message from God to remind us that the earth will never again be destroyed by a flood of water.

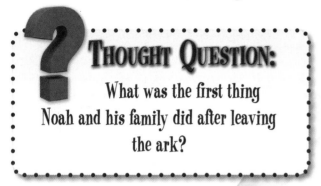

THOUGHT QUESTION:

What was the first thing Noah and his family did after leaving the ark?

Chapter 3

ABRAHAM'S GREATEST TEST

Genesis 22

If you have a friend who always keeps his word, you know you can depend on him when you're in trouble. Abraham had found God to be just such a friend.

Abraham grew up in a city named Ur—one of the oldest cities mentioned in the Bible. It was located near the Euphrates river, in the land that is now called Iraq. Much of the city was built with bricks baked from clay. These bricks were so strong that pieces of the ancient city walls of Ur are still standing.

The people in Ur worshiped idols and prayed in temples of the moon god. But Abraham worshiped the true God of heaven—the God who created the earth and everything in it. Abraham refused to worship idols of wood or stone. God loved faithful Abraham and wanted to protect him and his family from the evil ways of the people around them. So God told Abraham to leave Ur and move far way to a land called Canaan.

Abraham did what God told him. He loaded all his belonging on the backs of camels and donkeys and carts. He gathered all his flocks of sheep and herds of cows. Then, moving slowly, Abraham and his family left Ur where they had lived all their lives. They finally came to the land of Canaan and settled there.

Years passed, and Abraham grew older. In fact, he was more than one hundred years old when this story happened! During all these years, God had protected his friend and blessed him. As a result, Abraham had become very wealthy. Thousands of his sheep fed on the grass-covered hills, and hundreds of his servants and their families lived nearby in tents.

GOD SAYS:

" 'Take now your son, your only son Isaac, whom you love, and go to the land of Moriah, and offer him there as a burnt offering on one of the mountains.' "
–Genesis 22:2

But Abraham's greatest happiness was being with his son Isaac, who had grown to be a strong, healthy young man. Abraham depended on Isaac to help care for his flocks and herds and to deal with the servants. God had promised to give all the land of Canaan to Abraham and to his descendants. Abraham knew that if Isaac was to possess the land of Canaan as God had said, he must become a strong, dependable leader.

One night while Abraham stood outside his tent watching the stars, the Lord spoke to him again. "Abraham!" He said.

"Here am I," said Abraham.

"Take now your son," said the Lord, "your only son Isaac, whom you love, and go to the land of Moriah, and offer him there as a burnt offering on one of the mountains of which I shall tell you."

Abraham had trusted God all his life; surely He would not fail him now. But why would the Lord ask him to do such a terrible thing? Wasn't Isaac the son who was to inherit the promised country of Canaan? If he were killed, how would Abraham's family ever possess that beautiful land?

On the other hand, Abraham trusted God completely. He had followed Him all His life. He knew God would never lead Him in the wrong way. Abraham determined that he would obey God no matter what.

Early the next morning Abraham awakened Isaac and two of his servants and told them they were going on a trip with him to offer sacrifices. Isaac had often gone with his father to worship God, so he wasn't surprised his father asked him to go on such a journey with him. The servants chopped wood, tied it in bundles, and placed it on a donkey. With no matches in those days, they probably had to carry hot coals of fire in a pot.

The father and son set out on their journey to the land of Moriah, to the place where the city of Jerusalem would someday be built. They did not awaken Sarah to tell her goodbye, because Abraham was afraid if he told his wife the sad news, she would stop him from obeying God.

The land of Moriah was about fifty miles from their home in Beersheba, and it was not until the morning of the third day of travel that Abraham saw the mountain where he was to make the sacrifice. When they came to the foot of the mountain, Abraham told his servants to stay there with the donkey. Pointing to the mountaintop, the father said, "The lad and I will go yonder and worship, and we will come back to you."

The servants waited with the pack animal, and the father and son began climbing the mountain together. Isaac carried the heavy bundle of wood, while his father carried the knife and the fire.

Noticing that they had no lamb to offer on the altar, Isaac stopped. He thought his father had forgotten to bring a sacrifice. "My father!" said Isaac to Abraham.

"Here I am, my son," Abraham responded.

"Look, the fire and the wood," he said, "but where is the lamb for a burnt offering?"

"My son, God will provide for Himself the lamb for a burnt offering," said

QUICK FACT:

Isaac could easily have escaped; he was much stronger than old Abraham. Instead, Isaac allowed his father to lay him on the altar and tie his hands and feet.

Abraham. He didn't have the heart to tell Isaac that *he* was to be the sacrifice! Then the father and the son continued their climb.

Finally the two came to the place where God had directed that the altar was to be built. They gathered stones and piled them up to make the altar. Then they carefully arranged the wood on the stones. When there was nothing more to prepare, Abraham told Isaac about God's command. The young man listened to his father. At first, no doubt, he was unable to believe his ears. But he loved and trusted his father. And he loved and trusted God. Isaac could easily have run away if he wanted to. But he was willing to obey and to be the sacrifice. He allowed his father to lay him on the altar and to tie his hands and feet.

The hour of greatest test had come to Abraham. He knew that the people who worshiped the sun god in the land of Ur sometimes offered their children as sacrifices to idols, but the true God had never made such a terrible request before. Yet, even in this awful moment, Abraham did not disobey God. He lifted the knife to kill his own son.

As he raised his hand ready to strike, a Voice called from heaven: "Abraham! Abraham!"

"Here I am," he replied.

"Do not lay your hand on the lad," the Voice said, "or do anything to him; for now I know that you fear God, since you have not withheld your son, your only son, from Me."

Abraham could have shouted for joy. His son was safe! His love and loyalty to God had been severely tested, but he had proved true and faithful.

Then Abraham saw in the bushes a ram caught by its horns. So he grabbed the animal and offered it as a sacrifice to the Lord. He named that place Jehovah-jireh, which means "The Lord will provide."

THOUGHT QUESTION: Why did God tell Abraham to kill his own son?

A very happy father and son hiked down the mountain together and met the waiting servants! For Abraham and Isaac, the sun shone brighter and the birds sang more sweetly than ever before. Soon they were on their way home to Beersheba.

It had been the most difficult test Abraham had ever faced. But he had trusted God, and once more God had rewarded his faithfulness.

It had a been a great test for young Isaac, as well. He must have realized as never before that God had special work for him to do, because his life had been so wonderfully spared.

Chapter 4

JOSEPH, THE DREAMER

Genesis 37; 39–41

Joseph, the great-great-grandson of Abraham, had eleven brothers—ten older brothers and one younger brother. Joseph's ten older brothers were not good men. They were selfish and quarrelsome, and often they told lies and deceived their father. When Joseph saw his brothers doing wrong, he tried to get them to do right. But they hated him for his words of reproof.

To show Joseph how much he loved him, Jacob gave him a beautiful robe with many bright colors woven into it. It was a special honor for Joseph, but when his ten brothers saw him in the beautiful coat, they hated him all the more.

One night Joseph had a dream. The next morning he told it to his brothers. He said, "There we were, binding sheaves in the field. Then behold, my sheaf arose and also stood upright; and indeed your sheaves stood all around and bowed down to my sheaf."

His brothers said scornfully, "Shall you indeed reign over us? Or shall you indeed have dominion over us?"

A few nights later, Joseph had a second dream, and again he told it to his brothers. He told them that in this dream he saw the sun, moon, and eleven stars bowing before him.

Joseph's older brothers felt jealous. They hated him more and more because of his dreams and because he was proud of his beautiful coat. When Jacob heard of his son's dreams, he wondered if God was telling the family that Joseph would someday become someone great.

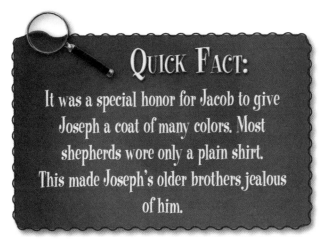

Not long after this, Joseph's older brothers were taking care of their flocks some miles from home. Joseph went to see how they were doing. When they saw Joseph coming, they said to each other, "Look, this dreamer is coming! Come therefore, let us now kill him and cast him into some pit; and we shall say, 'Some wild beast has devoured him.' We shall see what will become of his dreams!"

But they didn't kill Joseph. Instead, they sold him as a slave to a band of Ishmaelite traders who were passing by. As the Ishmaelites' caravan disappeared over the hills, there must have been some guilty looks on the faces of the brothers. They had sold their younger brother to be a slave!

But God was watching over Joseph even in this hour of trouble. Joseph prayed for God's help, and he determined to do what was right no matter what happened.

The Ishmaelites took Joseph to Egypt and sold him to Potiphar, the captain of the king's guard. Egypt presented many strange sights to Joseph. He saw temples, great pyramids, and swift sail boats on the Nile River. Joseph did his work so well that

Potiphar put him in charge of his house and all his property. God was with Joseph, and the king's officer was pleased to find a slave who could be trusted.

For ten years Joseph worked in Potiphar's house. Potiphar's wife hated Joseph because he was faithful to God and refused to do wrong. She lied about him and had Joseph thrown into prison.

The young man sat in a dark cell for days and weeks. But in spite of this unfair punishment, Joseph still determined to obey God.

One day great excitement arose at the prison. Two important officials of the palace—the king's butler and baker—were imprisoned by order of Pharaoh, the Egyptian ruler. Joseph was given the task of caring for the new prisoners. One morning when he came to visit the butler and the baker in

their cell, he saw that they were unhappy. "Why do you look so sad today?" he asked.

"We each have had a dream," they replied, "and there is no interpreter of it."

Joseph said to them, "Do not interpretations belong to God? Tell them to me, please."

So the butler of Pharaoh told Joseph his dream. "Behold, in my dream," he said, "a vine was before me, and in the vine were three branches; it was as though it budded, its blossoms shot forth, and its clusters brought forth ripe grapes. Then Pharaoh's cup was in my hand; and I took the grapes and pressed them into Pharaoh's cup, and placed the cup in Pharaoh's hand."

Joseph listened closely. He remembered the dreams he had had as a teenager. God immediately made the meaning of this dream clear to him. Joseph told the butler that the dream meant that Pharaoh would restore him to his position at court in three days.

The baker, too, was anxious to find out what his dream meant. "In my dream," he said, "there were three white baskets on my head. In the uppermost basket were all kinds of baked goods for Pharaoh, and the birds ate them out of the basket on my head."

When Joseph heard the dream, he was sad. But he courageously told the baker the truth. He told the baker that his dream meant that Pharaoh would put him to death in three days!

Three days later, it all happened just as God had told Joseph it would. Pharaoh restored the butler to his position, and he hung the baker.

Joseph asked the king's butler to remember him and put in a good word for him with Pharaoh. But days, weeks, and months dragged by, and nothing happened. Joseph had done nothing wrong. When would his prayers be answered? Would he ever be set free from this Egyptian prison?

One morning, excitement and confusion spread through Pharaoh's palace because of two strange dreams the king had dreamed the night before. The dreams seemed to contain a special message for

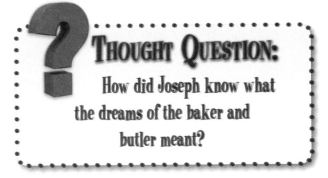

THOUGHT QUESTION:
How did Joseph know what the dreams of the baker and butler meant?

him, but Pharaoh couldn't understand what the dreams meant. He asked all the wise men of his court to explain his dreams, but they couldn't.

Suddenly the butler remembered how Joseph had told him the meaning of his dream in prison two years earlier. Quickly the butler told Pharaoh about Joseph.

The king was desperate to find anyone who could tell him the truth. Royal messengers ran to the prison and ordered the jailer to release Joseph and bring him to the palace. Soon Joseph was standing before Pharaoh who sat on a golden throne! It was a breathtaking moment for Joseph, but he stood fearlessly awaiting the king's words.

"I have had a dream," Pharaoh said to Joseph, "and there is no one who can interpret it. But I have heard it said of you that you can understand a dream, to interpret it."

"God will give Pharaoh an answer of peace," Joseph answered, making sure that the king understood he did not have wisdom in himself to interpret the dreams.

Then the ruler said, "In my dream, I stood on the bank of the river. Suddenly seven cows came up out of the river, fine looking and fat; and they fed in the meadow. Then behold, seven other cows came up after them, poor and very ugly and gaunt, such ugliness as I have never seen in all the land of Egypt. And the gaunt and ugly cows ate up the first seven, the fat cows. When they had eaten them up, no one would have known that they had eaten them, for they were just as ugly as at the beginning. So I awoke.

> **GOD SAYS:**
> "So Joseph answered Pharaoh, saying, 'It is not in me; God will give Pharaoh an answer of peace.'" –Genesis 41:16

"Also I saw in my dream, and suddenly seven heads [of grain] came up on one stalk, full and good. Then behold, seven heads [of grain], withered, thin, and blighted by the east wind, sprang up after them. And the thin heads devoured the seven good heads."

Joseph told Pharaoh that his two dreams had the same meaning. The seven fat cows and the seven plump ears of grain represented the next seven years, when Egypt would have good crops and rich harvests. But after that would come seven

Joseph, the Dreamer

years of terrible famine. God was showing Pharaoh what was about to happen.

Pharaoh listened carefully. He saw in this prisoner a man of strength and ability, a man who had faith in God. Joseph continued speaking: "Now therefore, let Pharaoh select a discerning and wise man, and set him over the land of Egypt. Let Pharaoh do this, and let him appoint officers over the land, to collect one-fifth of the produce of the land of Egypt in the seven plentiful years. And let them gather all the food of those good years that are coming, and store up grain under the authority of Pharaoh, and let them keep food in the cities. Then that food shall be as a reserve for the land for the seven years of famine which shall be in the land of Egypt, that the land may not perish during the famine."

Pharaoh thought for a moment and then said to Joseph, "You shall be over my house, and all my people shall be ruled according to your word; only in regard to the throne will I be greater than you. . . . See, I have set you over all the land of Egypt."

Joseph must have felt as if he were in a dream. Only a few hours before, he had been sitting in the dark dungeon, and now he was a royal official second only to Pharaoh himself!

As the new governor of the land, Joseph rode in a royal chariot drawn by stately horses. Servants ran before him shouting for the people to bow in homage to him.

During the next seven years the land was filled with plenty. Joseph built large storehouses and filled them with so much grain that he couldn't keep track of it all. Then when the seven years of abundant crops had passed, the famine came just as God had told Pharaoh it would.

QUICK FACT:

God was able to use Joseph to not only save all Egypt from starvation, but his family back in Canaan too.

The hungry Egyptians came to Joseph. He opened the huge storehouses and sold them grain. So Joseph's years of hard work and planning saved the nation from starvation.

Joseph must have thought about the dreams he had dreamed many years before when he was a teenager—of his brothers' sheaves of grain bowing to his sheaf and of the sun, moon, and stars bowing before him. His brothers had mocked him and hated him because of his dreams. But they had come true. Joseph was the second most important person in the most powerful nation on earth at that time. God had blessed him because he was faithful in all things. And through Joseph, God was blessing all the people of Egypt and the surrounding nations with food during the time of famine.

Chapter 5

THE WALLS OF JERICHO FALL DOWN

Joshua 1:1–7:1

Moses had delivered God's people, the Israelites, from captivity in Egypt and had led them to the borders of Canaan, the land God had promised to Abraham and his descendants. But they didn't trust God so they couldn't enter until a new generation grew up who was ready to follow God and possess the land.

Now, some forty years later, the Israelites stood, once again, on the banks of the Jordan River. They could look across and see the Promised Land, on the other side. Meanwhile, Moses had died, and God had asked Joshua to complete the task of bringing His people into the Promised Land.

The first thing Joshua did was to send two men into Jericho, the city just across the river. These men would be spies to study the situation. They slipped into Jericho and walked along the narrow streets, feeling strange among foreign people. Before long, curious men began to follow them to see where they were going. Someone hurried away to tell the ruler of Jericho that spies from the camp of Israel were in town.

The spies quickly turned in at an open doorway and met a woman named Rahab. She welcomed them when they told her that they were Israelites. "I know that the Lord has given you the land," she said to the spies, "that the terror of you has fallen on us, and that all the inhabitants of the land are fainthearted because of you."

Soon officers arrived at Rahab's house and said to her, "Bring out the men who have come to you, who have entered your house, for they have come to search out all the country."

Rahab admitted that the spies had been in her house, but she told the officers the two men had already left. Actually, she had hidden them under piles of flax that were drying on the flat roof of her house. When the officers had gone, she told the men, "Now therefore, I beg you, swear to me by the Lord, since I have shown you kindness, that you also will show kindness to my father's house, and give me a true token, and spare my father, my mother, my brothers, my sisters, and all that they have, and deliver our lives from death."

The men replied, "Our lives for yours, if none of you tell this business of ours. And it shall be, when the Lord has given us the land, that we will deal kindly and truly with you."

Because she had spared their lives, the men told Rahab to bring all her family—father, mother, brothers, and sisters—into her house and to put a scarlet cord in her window. They promised her that when they destroyed the city, they would spare her family.

Rahab's house was built on the wide city wall. When it was dark, she let the two spies down to the ground outside the city by a rope from her window. The two men returned to the camp of Israel and reported to Joshua, "Truly the Lord has delivered all the land into our hands for indeed all the inhabitants of the country are fainthearted because of us."

The next morning the people marched to the banks of the Jordan River not far from Jericho. Three days later, the leaders told the people to be ready to advance when they saw the priests pick up the ark—a sacred golden box containing the Ten Commandments.

At a signal from Joshua, the priests marched forward with the ark, and the people followed in orderly procession behind them. There were no bridges, and at that time of year the river was flooded from bank to bank. Crossing the Jordan looked impossible. But as soon as priests' feet touched the muddy waters of the river, the water plunging toward them from upstream came to a stop and formed a wall. The water that was rushing by kept flowing downstream, leaving dry ground so that the people could cross over safely.

The priests carried the ark into the middle of the dry river bed and stopped. There they waited until all the people with their cows and sheep and goats had marched past them and reached the other side. Then the priests went to the far side of the river, and the water started flowing normally again!

The Israelites had finally entered the Promised Land!

God instructed Joshua: "See! I have given Jericho into your hand, its king, and the mighty men of valor. You shall march around the city, all you men of war; you shall go all around the city once." They were to march around Jericho once a day for six days, with priests carrying the ark and seven priests holding a ram's horn. On the seventh day the army would march around the city seven times, while the seven priests blew the horns. After the seventh time, the priests would blow a long blast on the horns, and when the people heard it, all

> ## GOD SAYS:
> " 'See! I have given Jericho into your hand, its king, and the mighty men of valor.' " –Joshua 6:2

of them at once would raise a mighty shout. At that moment the wall of the city would fall down so that the Israelites could march right in.

When Joshua heard this instruction, he was very pleased with God's plan for taking the walled city. He called the priests and commanded them to prepare to carry the ark and also to appoint seven priests who would carry rams' horns. They were to start marching around the city of Jericho immediately.

THOUGHT QUESTION:

Can we hide anything from God?

The people of Jericho were afraid. They closed and barred the city gates. No one could enter, and no one could leave. Every morning Rahab went to the window facing the countryside to make sure the scarlet cord was in plain sight. Looking out her window, she could see the soldiers of Jericho with their swords and spears, guarding the wall.

One morning Rahab heard rams' horns sounding in the distance. Soon a strange procession appeared. A column of Israelite soldiers was leading the procession, and priests dressed in white came marching behind, carrying a box covered by a big cloth. In the morning sunlight the soldiers' armor shone in rich splendor. Behind the ark came more soldiers in full battle gear.

Seven priests were blowing their rams' horns, and the sound echoed through the valley. Around the walled city, the men of Israel marched. After they had circled the city, all was quiet. The procession disappeared in the direction of the Israelite camp.

Rahab wondered what might happen next. Would the soldiers attack the city? Would Rahab and her family be spared, as the spies had promised?

The next morning the soldiers and priests came marching again. Every morning for six days, Rahab saw the same column of men go marching by. The soldiers of Jericho, looking down from the wall, began to make jokes about the men of Israel and said that they were afraid to fight.

During the week, Rahab had gathered her relatives into her house. On the seventh morning Rahab and her family watched the soldiers marching by, and the priests carrying the ark. On this day, however, the procession didn't stop when it had gone around the city. It kept on marching, marching, marching until it had circled the wall of Jericho seven times.

Then the priests blew their horns, and the vast throng of Israel, who had gathered nearby, gave a mighty shout. The shout echoed through the valley and mingled with a terrible rumbling. As the shout died away, the rumbling grew louder and louder. The walls of Jericho shook and then crumbled and fell with a thunderous roar! The soldiers of Israel ran forward and quickly overtook the city, killing all the people and taking the silver and gold for the Lord's treasury. They burned every building except Rahab's house. Joshua commanded the spies, "Bring the woman out of it, with all that belong to her, as you swore to her."

When the two spies arrived at Rahab's house, they found her and all her family waiting for them. Rahab was welcomed in the camp of Israel, because the people had heard how she saved the lives of the spies. Rahab believed in God, and later she married a man of Israel named Salmon. She became the great-great-grandmother of David, king of Israel.

Chapter 6

A Battle With Pitchers and Torches

Judges 6; 7

After years of peace and prosperity, the people of Israel began to worship idols, and God permitted the armies of Midian to overrun Israel. No one was safe in his house or in the field. Midianites were everywhere. The attacks became so bad that the Israelites fled to caves and other places in the mountains—any place they could hide from the enemy. For seven years the invaders swarmed over the country like grasshoppers, ruining the farms and houses. In this time of trouble the people remembered the Lord and called on Him for help. He sent a prophet through the country with a message:

"Thus says the Lord God of Israel: 'I brought you up from Egypt and brought you out of the house of bondage; and I delivered you out of the hand of the Egyptians and out of the hand of all who oppressed you, and drove them out before you and gave you their land. Also I said to you, "I am the Lord your God; do not fear the gods of the Amorites, in whose land you dwell." But you have not obeyed My voice.' "

Soon after this, a young man of the tribe of Manasseh, who was loyal to God, was threshing some wheat. Gideon was keeping the grain hidden from the Midianites, because if they found it they would take it from him. While he was at work, an angel appeared and said to him, "The Lord is with you, you mighty man of valor!"

"O my lord," Gideon replied, "if the Lord is with us, why then has all this happened to us? And where are all His miracles which our fathers told us about, saying, 'Did not the Lord bring us up from Egypt?' But now the Lord has forsaken us and delivered us into the hands of the Midianites."

JOE MANISCALCO

Then God Himself spoke to Gideon. "Go in this [strength] of yours, and you shall save Israel from the hand of the Midianites. Have I not sent you?"

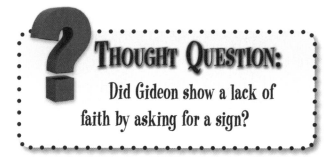

THOUGHT QUESTION:

Did Gideon show a lack of faith by asking for a sign?

"O my Lord, how can I save Israel?" Gideon asked. "Indeed my clan is the weakest in Manasseh, and I am the least in my father's house."

"Surely I will be with you," the Lord assured him, "and you shall defeat the Midianites as one man."

Soon the Midianites and the Amalekites gathered all their fighting men and marched toward Israel. They set up camp in the Valley of Jezreel. At that time, the Spirit of God filled young Gideon with great courage. He blew a trumpet, calling the people around him to arms. He sent messengers to the tribes of Manasseh, Asher, Zebulun, and Naphtali asking for army volunteers.

Gideon decided he needed more proof that God would be with him in battle. He said to the Lord, "If You will save Israel by my hand as You have said—look, I shall put a fleece of wool on the threshing floor; if there is dew on the fleece only, and it is dry on all the ground, then I shall know that You will save Israel by my hand, as You have said."

The next morning he got up early and went to find the fleece. It was so wet that he wrung out a bowlful of water from it; but the ground was dry.

Gideon still wasn't completely sure, so he said to God, "Do not be angry with me, but let me speak just once more: Let me test, I pray, just once more with the fleece; let it now be dry only on the fleece, but on all the ground let there be dew."

He hurried out of his tent the next morning and found heavy dew on the ground, but the fleece was dry. Now Gideon was sure of his mission. He knew he faced a powerful enemy, but God had promised the victory even though the Israelite army was much smaller and not as well equipped. Gideon was ready to advance by faith.

Gideon was making plans to attack the Midianites when God gave him a strange message. The Lord said, "The people who are with you are too many for Me to give the Midianites into their hands, lest Israel claim glory for itself against Me, saying, 'My own hand has saved me.' Now therefore, proclaim in the hearing of the people, saying, 'Whoever is fearful and afraid, let him turn and depart at once from Mount Gilead.' "

Calling all his volunteer soldiers together, Gideon told them what God had said. His heart sank as he saw twenty-two thousand men pick up their weapons and start for their homes. Only ten thousand men stayed to attack the hundreds of thousands of the enemy.

But the Lord said to Gideon, "The people are still too many; bring them down to the water, and I will test them for you there. Then it will be, that of whom I say to you, 'This one shall go with you,' the same shall go with you; and of whomever I say to you, 'This one shall not go with you,' the same shall not go."

Gideon marched his men down to the river, and God told him to watch them drink. Some of the men hurried across the stream toward the enemy camp, lapping up water as they advanced. But most of them knelt by the riverbank and drank in a leisurely way. Only three hundred men quickly lapped the water with their tongues. God said to Gideon, "By the three hundred men who lapped I will save you, and deliver the Midianites into your hand. Let all the other people go, every man to his place."

Sadly, Gideon ordered another nine thousand seven hundred soldiers to return to their homes! How would he fight the Midianites with just a handful of warriors?

That night Gideon and his servant went to spy on the enemy camp. The Midianites were spread out in the valley like a huge horde of locusts. Gideon crept up to the side of one of the enemy tents, and he heard two men talking. One said, "I have had a dream: To my surprise, a loaf of barley bread tumbled into the camp of Midian; it came to a tent and struck it so that it fell and overturned, and the tent collapsed."

The other said, "This is nothing else but the sword of Gideon the son of Joash, a man of Israel! Into his hand God has delivered Midian and the whole camp."

GOD SAYS:

"The Lord said to Gideon, 'The people who are with you are too many for Me to give the Midianites into their hands.' " –Judges 7:2

37

Gideon prayed a silent prayer of thanks to God and then slipped away and returned to his camp. As soon as he got back, he gave the command: "Arise, for the Lord has delivered the camp of Midian into your hand!"

Gideon divided his force of three hundred men into three groups. The men tried to look like soldiers ready to fight, although the only equipment they had was an empty pitcher with a torch inside, and a trumpet.

QUICK FACT:

God delivered the Midianites into the hand of Gideon and his three hundred men.

"Look at me," Gideon said to his men, "and do likewise; watch, and when I come to the edge of the camp you shall do as I do: When I blow the trumpet, I and all who are with me, then you also blow the trumpets on every side of the whole camp, and say, 'The sword of the Lord and of Gideon!' "

Quietly the three groups of men advanced and surrounded the vast camp of Midian. At a signal from their commander, the three hundred men blew their trumpets and broke their pitchers. The torches gleamed brightly in the darkness. Then they shouted, "The sword of the Lord and of Gideon!"

The sleeping army woke up in terror. They saw gleaming torches everywhere, and the noise of the trumpets was deafening. Believing they were far outnumbered, the soldiers of Midian jumped up and ran. In the darkness and confusion they bumped into each other and began to fight and kill their own companions. As the Midianite army fled, Gideon sent messengers to the surrounding territory to call for volunteers to chase the Midianites and destroy their forces.

A great victory came to Israel, not by the strength of the sword, but by the power of God.

Chapter 7

A Strong Weak Man

Judges 13–16

Israel forgot about God. He withdrew His protection, and the idol-worshiping Philistines invaded Israel and oppressed God's people.

Monoah was an Israelite who was faithful to God. He and his wife did not have any children. An angel appeared to them and told them they would have a son. The boy, he said, should never drink alcohol nor eat unclean food. He must allow his hair to grow and never cut it. Then the angel promised: "He shall begin to deliver Israel out of the hand of the Philistines."

His mother named the child Samson. He grew very strong, because God's Spirit was with him. But when Samson grew to be a sturdy young man, he became restless. He went to Timnah, across the border in the land of the Philistines. There he fell in love with a girl and wanted to marry her.

His parents urged him to marry an Israelite girl, a young woman who loved and worshiped the true God. But Samson insisted. He told his father, "Get her for me, for she pleases me well."

Once, while Samson was on his way to visit the girl, a young lion rushed at him and attacked him. The Spirit of God came over Samson, and he grabbed the savage beast and tore it apart with his bare hands! But he didn't tell anyone what he had done.

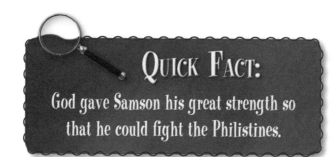

QUICK FACT:
God gave Samson his great strength so that he could fight the Philistines.

Later, Samson saw the body of the lion he had killed. In the carcass, he found a swarm of bees. He scraped out some of the honey and ate it as he walked along.

Soon after this, Samson married the Philistine woman; among the wedding guests were thirty young men. Samson said to them, "Let me pose a riddle to you. If you can correctly solve and explain it to me within the seven days of the feast, then I will give you thirty linen garments and thirty changes of clothing. But if you cannot explain it to me, then you shall give me thirty linen garments and thirty changes of clothing."

"Pose your riddle," they said, "that we may hear it."

So he said to them,

"Out of the eater came something to eat,
And out of the strong came something sweet."

For three days the young men thought about the riddle, but they couldn't come up with the answer. On the fourth day of the feast, they threatened Samson's wife: "Entice your husband, that he may explain the riddle to us, or else we will burn you and your father's house with fire."

So Samson's wife cried and begged him to tell her the answer. After seven days of her tears, he told her the secret. She immediately went to the young men and gave them the answer to the riddle.

The thirty men came to Samson and said,

"What is sweeter than honey?
And what is stronger than a lion?"

Samson was furious. The Spirit of God came over him. He went to Ashkelon, a Philistine city, and killed thirty men, stripping them of their clothing. Then he returned to Timnah and gave the garments to the young Philistines to fulfill his bargain. He was so angry, however, that he went back to his father's house, not stopping to see his wife.

A Strong Weak Man

After Samson's anger cooled, and he went to visit his wife. When he arrived, his father-in-law said, "I really thought that you thoroughly hated her." And he told Samson that he had given his daughter to another man.

Now the strong young giant was really mad! He said, "This time I shall be blameless regarding the Philistines if I harm them."

He went out into the hills and caught three hundred foxes and tied them in pairs with a torch between their tails. The he lit the torches and turned a hundred fifty pairs of foxes loose in the Philistines' fields. The foxes ran through the wheat fields, setting on them fire along with the vineyards and the olive groves.

In revenge the Philistines set fire to the house where Samson's wife lived and burned her and her father to death. When he found out about his wife's death, Samson attacked the men of Timnah and killed many of them.

Samson! The very name struck terror into the hearts of the Philistines because he had done so much damage to their nation in such a short time. But when they tried to capture him, he seized the jawbone of a donkey lying nearby on the ground, and killed a thousand Philistines! Another time Samson escaped the Philistines by pulling up the city gates and carrying them off on his shoulders!

For some twenty years Samson continued to be the judge of Israel. But once again he fell in love with a Philistine woman. Her name was Delilah.

The Philistine rulers came to her and said, "Entice him, and find out where his great strength lies."

Delilah went to Samson and begged, "Please tell me where your great strength lies, and with what you may be bound to afflict you."

Samson replied, "If they bind me with seven fresh bowstrings, not yet dried, then I shall become weak, and be like any other man."

Delilah told the Philistine rulers what he had said. They brought seven bowstrings to her, and she tied Samson with them. But when the rulers tried to capture him, Samson snapped the bowstrings as if they were threads.

Then Delilah said to Samson, "Look, you have mocked me and told me lies. Now, please tell me what you may be bound with."

GOD SAYS:

" 'If I am shaven, then my strength will leave me, and I shall become weak, and be like any other man.' " -Judges 16:17

Samson told her that if he were bound with new ropes, he would be powerless. But this wasn't true either.

Next Samson told her that if his hair were woven into the web of a loom, he would lose all his strength. But that wasn't true, and a third time she failed to find out his secret.

The foolish man should have seen that Delilah was trying to betray him to his enemies. But she kept begging and whining and complaining until at last Samson told her the truth.

"No razor has ever come upon my head," he said. "If I am shaven, then my strength will leave me, and I shall become weak, and be like any other man."

She lulled her husband to sleep on her lap, and then she cut off all his hair. Then she cried out, "The Philistines are upon you, Samson!"

Samson woke up and thought, *I will go out as before, at other times, and shake myself free!* He didn't realize that his hair had been cut, that his strength had vanished, and that the Spirit of God had left him. The evil Philistines seized Samson, gouged out his eyes, and took him to Gaza. Poor blind giant! Now Samson was a helpless prisoner. He was forced to spend his days pushing on the bar of a large grindstone to grind grain, like a slave.

But what happens after a haircut? Samson's hair began to grow back! And as his hair grew, so did his great strength.

To celebrate Samson's capture, the Philistines held a lavish feast. During the feast, they shouted, "Call for Samson, that he may perform for us." Soon a boy appeared, leading the blind, unsteady giant. When Samson's enemies saw him, they laughed and jeered.

Samson told the boy who was leading him, "Let me feel the pillars which support the temple, so that I can lean on them."

The hall was filled with the Philistine rulers and leading people—about three thousand men and women altogether. Samson bowed his head and prayed to the God of heaven, saying, "O Lord God, remember me, I pray! Strengthen me, I pray, just this once, O God, that I may with one blow take vengeance on the Philistines for my two eyes!"

This was the man's last prayer. He braced himself against the two great pillars that supported the roof of the hall.

"Let me die with the Philistines!" Samson said, and with all his might he pushed on the pillars. As they fell, the roof tumbled down with a terrible crash on all the people below. "So the dead that he killed at his death were more than he had killed in his life," the Bible says.

THOUGHT QUESTION:

Why did God give Samson his strength back?

Samson, who could not control his own habits and desires, might have written a much longer and more heroic chapter in the history of his people if he had always been true to God. But he forgot that the greatness of a man is measured not by physical ability but by self-control and obedience to the Spirit of God.

Chapter 8

RUTH, GREAT-GRANDMOTHER OF A KING

Ruth 1–4

Famine struck the land of Canaan during the days of the judges. The parched ground baked in the hot sun; grain shriveled in the stalk. Fruit withered and fell from the trees, and the grass became brown in the pasture.

Elimelech, a man of the tribe of Judah, lived in Bethlehem with his wife, Naomi. They had two sons, Mahlon and Chilion. When the crops failed and famine spread through the land, Elimelech decided to move southeast across the Jordan River to the land of Moab. In that foreign country the family lived for ten years. The two sons married young women of Moab. One was named Orpah, the other Ruth.

Trouble came to the family during this time. Elimelech died, and soon afterward his two sons became sick and died as well. This left Naomi a widow in a foreign land with only her two daughters-in-law. She decided to return to her home in Bethlehem, because she had heard that the famine in Canaan was over.

As Naomi started on her journey home, Ruth and Orpah accompanied her. But when Naomi thought about the future for the two young widows, she said, "Go, return each to her mother's house. The Lord deal kindly with you, as you have dealt with the dead and with me. The Lord grant that you may find rest, each in the house of her husband."

She kissed the two young women goodbye, and they began to cry. They said, "Surely we will return with you to your people."

Naomi replied, "Turn back, my daughters; why will you go with me?"

Orpah said goodbye to her mother-in-law and returned to her own people. But Ruth had faith in the God of heaven, and she loved her mother-in-law. She said to Naomi,

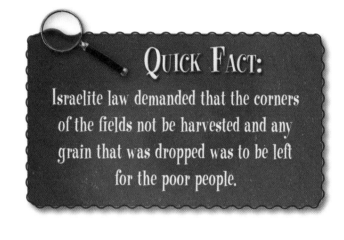

QUICK FACT:
Israelite law demanded that the corners of the fields not be harvested and any grain that was dropped was to be left for the poor people.

"Entreat me not to leave you,
  Or to turn back from following
    after you;
For wherever you go, I will go;
And wherever you lodge, I will
  lodge;
Your people shall be my people,
And your God, my God."

The two women made the journey to Bethlehem, where they were greeted by Naomi's relatives and friends.

Naomi and Ruth found a home in Bethlehem at the beginning of the barley harvest. The laws of Israel required the owners of grain fields to allow poor people to glean the stalks of grain left behind by the reapers. They could also have the grain that grew in the corners of the fields.

Although the two women had a place to live, they needed food to eat. Ruth, knowing the law of the harvest, said to Naomi, "Please let me go to the field, and glean heads of grain after him in whose sight I may find favor."

So Ruth went to glean in the field of Boaz, a wealthy relative of Naomi's husband. While Ruth was picking up the grain that had fallen from the hands of the reapers, Boaz entered the field. He saw the beautiful woman and wondered who she was.

"Whose young woman is this?" Boaz asked the servant in charge of the harvesters.

"It is the young Moabite woman who came back with Naomi from the country of Moab," the servant answered.

Boaz walked over to Ruth and said, "You will listen, my daughter, will you not? Do not go to glean in another field, nor go from here, but stay close by my young women. Let your eyes be on the field which they reap, and go after them. Have I not commanded the young men not to touch you? And when you are thirsty, go to the vessels and drink from what the young men have drawn."

Ruth bowed down to the ground before Boaz and asked him, "Why have I found favor in your eyes, that you should take notice of me, since I am a foreigner?"

"It has been fully reported to me," Boaz replied, "all that you have done for your mother-in-law since the death of your husband, and how you have left your father and your mother and the land of your birth, and have come to a people whom you did not know before."

Boaz could not forget Ruth's sweet smile. At mealtime the man said to her, "Come here, and eat of the bread, and dip your piece of bread in the vinegar." Ruth seated herself beside the gleaners, and Boaz gave her some of the roasted grain to eat.

After dinner, when Ruth had returned to her work, Boaz gave orders to his servants: "Let her glean even among the sheaves, and do not reproach her. Also let grain from the bundles fall purposely for her; leave it that she may glean, and do not rebuke her."

At sunset Ruth hurried home with the grain she had gathered. "Where have you gleaned today?" her mother-in-law asked. "And where did you work? Blessed be the one who took notice of you."

"The man's name with whom I worked today is Boaz," she said.

"This man is a relation of ours," Naomi said to her, "one of our close relatives." She added, "It is good, my daughter, that you go out with his young women, and that people do not meet you in any other field." Naomi hoped that Boaz would continue to look with favor upon the beautiful girl.

Although Boaz was a relative of Elimelech, another man in Bethlehem was a closer relative to Naomi's husband. According to the law of Israel, if a man died without leaving children, the nearest relative had the right to purchase the family property, and he could also marry the widow. If the nearest relative did not wish to buy the land, the next nearest relative could do so.

One day Boaz went to the city gate, where the town's business was conducted, and sat down. Soon the man who was the nearest relative of Naomi's husband came by. Boaz called to him and told him about the land that should be redeemed. "There is no one but you to redeem it," Boaz said, "and I am next after you."

"I will redeem it," the relative said.

Then Boaz said, "On the day you buy the field from the hand of Naomi, you must also buy it from Ruth the Moabitess, the wife of the dead, to perpetuate the name of the dead through his inheritance." This mean that whoever redeemed the land would also marry Ruth.

"I cannot redeem it for myself, lest I ruin my own inheritance," the man replied. "You redeem my right of redemption for yourself, for I cannot redeem it. . . . Buy it for yourself."

Then Boaz said to the city elders and the people standing by the gate, "You are witnesses this day that I have bought all that was Elimelech's, and all that was Chilion's and Mahlon's, from the hand of Naomi. Moreover, Ruth the

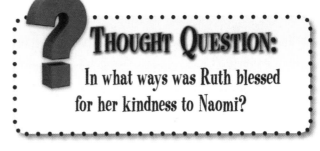

THOUGHT QUESTION: In what ways was Ruth blessed for her kindness to Naomi?

Moabitess, the widow of Mahlon, I have acquired as my wife, to perpetuate the name of the dead through his inheritance."

Naomi was very happy to see Ruth well married. Some time later the women of the neighborhood brought Naomi wonderful news. Ruth and Boaz had a baby son! The women said to Naomi, who was now a grandmother, "Blessed be the Lord, who has not left you this day without a close relative; and may his name be famous in Israel! And may he be to you a restorer of life and a nourisher of your old age."

Naomi went to Ruth's home and took the baby in her arms, rocking him tenderly. She became the baby's nurse, and she watched over him so lovingly that the neighborhood women teased her, saying, "There is a son born to Naomi."

The child's name was Obed. He became the grandfather of David, who became a mighty king of Israel.

Chapter 9

THE BOY PROPHET

1 Samuel 1–4

When the nation of Israel settled in Canaan, the temple, the beautiful tent where sacrifices were offered and God met with His people, was set up permanently at the city of Shiloh. Each year many of the faithful Israelites went there to worship God and to offer sacrifices and thank offerings.

Elkanah, a man from the town of Ramah, traveled to Shiloh to worship every year at the temple. He had two wives, Hannah and Peninnah, who accompanied him. Although Peninnah had children, she was jealous of Hannah, who was childless. Often when Elkanah wasn't around, Peninnah made mean, unkind remarks to Hannah and made her feel bad about having no sons or daughters. More than anything else she could think of, Hannah longed for a son.

One year when the family visited Shiloh, Hannah cried and was depressed. She hadn't eaten anything all day. In the evening, Elkanah told her how much he loved her. "Am I not better to you than ten sons?" he asked. But Hannah still wished with all her heart for a son. The next morning she went to the temple to pray. She made a vow to God that if she had a son, she would give him back to the Lord in service all the days of his life.

Eli, the high priest at the temple, saw Hannah standing near the entrance

with her eyes closed. Her lips were moving, but no sound came out of her mouth. At first Eli thought she was drunk, but Hannah said to him, "No, my lord, I am a woman of sorrowful spirit. . . . Out of the abundance of my complaint and grief I have spoken until now."

THOUGHT QUESTION:
Why did Hannah give Samuel away if she loved him so much?

Eli comforted her, saying, "Go in peace, and the God of Israel grant your petition which you have asked of Him." She returned to Elkanah's tent and ate with him. She felt better, and her face no longer looked so sad.

Sometime after the family returned to their home in Ramah, Hannah became pregnant and had a baby son. She was so happy! She named him Samuel, which means "Asked of God."

The years slipped by. When Samuel was old enough to leave home, Hannah kept her vow to God. She took the boy to the house of the Lord at Shiloh and presented him to Eli.

"O my lord!" she said to the high priest. "I am the woman who stood by you here, praying to the Lord. For this child I prayed, and the Lord has granted me my petition which I asked of Him. Therefore I also have lent him to the Lord; as long as he lives he shall be lent to the Lord." Elkanah's family worshiped God at the temple as they usually did, and Hannah prayed a beautiful prayer of thanks.

Little Samuel must have been homesick when his mother left him. Eli was an old man, and with all of the work to do in God's house, there was little time to play for a boy who lived with the high priest. But Samuel did his work faithfully. He opened the doors of the house of God in the morning and closed them in the evening. He kept the lamps trimmed, and he probably cleaned the floors and dusted the furniture in the rooms where the high priest lived.

Samuel wore a linen robe just like the one the priests wore as they served in the temple. Each year when Hannah came to worship at the Lord's house, she brought her son a new coat she had made with her own hands. Three more sons and two daughters were born to Hannah, so she wasn't lonely at home anymore.

Samuel slept in the temple near where the lamps burned in front of the golden ark. One night he was aroused from a sound sleep by a voice calling his name.

"Here I am!" he replied.

He thought the voice belonged to Eli, so he ran to the priest and said, "Here I am, for you called me."

"I did not call," Eli declared; "lie down again."

Samuel went back and lay down on his sleeping mat. Again a voice called out to him, "Samuel!"

Once more the boy arose and went to Eli's bed. "Here I am; for you called me," Samuel responded.

"I did not call, my son," replied the priest. "Go back and lie down."

When the voice called a third time, the boy got up quickly and went to Eli and said again, "Here I am, for you did call me."

Eli answered, "I did not call, my son; lie down again." Then Eli realized that it was the Lord calling the young boy. He said to Samuel, "Go, lie down; and it shall be, if He calls you, that you must say, 'Speak, Lord, for Your servant hears.'"

Until this time, Samuel had never received a message from God. The boy walked back to his bed and lay down. The Lord called again, "Samuel! Samuel!"

As Eli had told him to, Samuel said, "Speak, for Your servant hears."

Then the Lord spoke these words to Samuel: "Behold, I will do something in Israel at which both ears of everyone who hears it will tingle. In that day I will perform against Eli all that I have spoken concerning his house, from beginning to end. For I have told him that I will judge his house forever for the iniquity which he knows, because his sons made themselves vile, and he did not restrain them. And

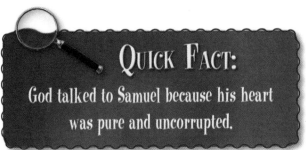

QUICK FACT:
God talked to Samuel because his heart was pure and uncorrupted.

therefore I have sworn to the house of Eli that the iniquity of Eli's house shall not be atoned for by sacrifice or offering forever."

In the morning when Samuel opened the double doors of the house of

GOD SAYS:

"So Samuel grew, and the Lord was with him and let none of his words fall to the ground." –1 Samuel 3:19

the Lord, Eli called the boy to him and said, "Samuel, my son!"

"Here I am," he answered.

"What is the word that the Lord spoke to you?" he asked. "Please do not hide it from me."

Then Samuel told the high priest everything that the Lord had told him.

"It is the Lord," Eli said. "Let Him do what seems good to Him."

Samuel had received his first message from God. There would be many more as he grew older. Samuel grew up to be a man who was true to God and obeyed all His commandments. God often gave him messages and instruction for the Israelites, and Samuel faithfully told the people what God had told him. Everyone in the nation came to realize that God had established Samuel as His prophet in Israel.

Chapter 10

DAVID THE GIANT SLAYER

1 Samuel 16; 17

Samuel was a prophet in Israel for many years. He led the people and helped them follow God. But the people wanted a king like the other nations around them. So God told Samuel to appoint Saul as Israel's king. But Saul failed to obey God, and at last, God decided Saul must be replaced with someone else.

"Fill your horn with oil and go," the Lord instructed Samuel; "I am sending you to Jesse the Bethlehemite. For I have provided Myself a king among his sons."

When Samuel came to Bethlehem he gathered the chief men of the town at the altar to worship God. Jesse and his sons were there. Now, Jesse was the son of Obed and grandson of Ruth, the young woman who had married Boaz. Jesse was a sheep rancher, and he had eight sons who helped him tend his flocks.

After Samuel had offered a sacrifice on the altar, he asked to see Jesse's sons. Beginning with Eliab, the oldest son, the prophet studied each of the young men carefully. He was pleased with Eliab's appearance, because he was strong and handsome. Samuel would have anointed him king of Israel right then, but the Lord said, "Do not look at his appearance or at his physical stature, because I have refused him. For the Lord does not see as man sees; for man looks at the outward appearance, but the Lord looks at the heart."

Next, Samuel looked carefully at Abinadab, the second-oldest son. Then sons three and four passed before him, but God didn't choose any of these as king. Then came sons five, six, and seven. But God did not choose them either. Now the prophet was troubled, and he said to Jesse, "The Lord has not chosen these . . . Are these all the young men?"

"There remains yet the youngest," Jesse replied, "and there he is, keeping the sheep."

"Send and bring him," said Samuel. "For we will not sit down till he comes here."

David the shepherd boy came in from the field and stood before Samuel. When the prophet saw the bright eyes and good-looking appearance of this teenager, he heard God say, "Arise, anoint him; for this is the one!" Samuel took the horn of oil and anointed the shepherd boy to be king, while his brothers and his father stood by and watched the strange ceremony.

In the meantime, Saul, Israel's king, had become even more sad and depressed. Though the king did not realize it, the Holy Spirit of God had left him for good. He began to show so many signs of mental illness that his servants suggested that soft harp music might soothe the king's troubled mind. Saul liked the suggestion and said, "Provide me now a man who can play well, and bring him to me."

One of the servants said, "Look, I have seen a son of Jesse the Bethlehemite, who is skillful in playing, a mighty man of valor, a man of war, prudent in speech, and a handsome person; and the Lord is with him."

Saul sent messengers to Jesse to tell him that David should come and play for him. So the father sent his boy to Saul's court. David played beautiful melodies on his harp, many of which he had composed while he herded sheep in the hills. Some of these songs are recorded in the Bible. Psalm 23 is a famous song of David.

Each time David played for him, Saul was refreshed by the music, and he felt happy again.

Meanwhile, the Philistines continued to attack the people of Israel. The enemy camped on one mountain, while Israel's army was stationed on another mountain across the Valley of Elah. Every day a mighty champion from the camp of the Philistines marched down into the valley and made fun of the Israelites. His name was Goliath, and he was a giant about nine feet, nine inches tall. He wore a helmet and a bronze coat of armor, and he carried a tall, heavy spear. His bronze coat alone weighed about 125 pounds. A soldier went in front of Goliath, carrying a shield. Every morning and evening for forty days, he stood before the soldiers of Israel, ridiculing them and shouting, "I defy the armies of Israel this day; give me a man, that we may fight together."

Whenever Saul and his soldiers heard the words of the Philistine, they were discouraged and afraid. Even though the king was tall and strong himself, he did not dare to fight the giant.

Three of David's older brothers were in the Israelite army. One day Jesse told David to go visit them in their camp. "See how your brothers fare," he told David, "and bring back news of them."

When David arrived at the camp he found everyone in a panic because of Goliath. When David heard that no Israelite soldier was willing to challenge the giant, David volunteered. He told King Saul, "Let no man's heart fail because of him; your servant will go and fight with this Philistine."

"You are not able to go against this Philistine to fight with him," said Saul to David, "for you are a youth, and he a man of war from his youth."

"Your servant used to keep his father's sheep," David replied, "and when a lion or a bear came and took a lamb

QUICK FACT:
David proved he was brave and faithful in his duties as a shepherd boy.

out of the flock, I went out after it and struck it, and delivered the lamb from its mouth; and when it arose against me, I caught it by its beard, and struck and killed it. Your servant has killed both lion and bear." Then David added these courageous words: "The Lord, who delivered me from the paw of the lion and from the paw of the bear, He will deliver me from the hand of this Philistine."

"Go," Saul agreed, "and the Lord be with you!" He had his servants place his own heavy armor on David. Then David fastened Saul's sword to the armor and tried to walk. He said, "I cannot walk with these, for I have not tested them." So he took off all the armor.

Picking up his shepherd's staff, and with only his sling in his other hand, David marched down to the stream in the middle of the valley and carefully chose five smooth stones. He put these in his leather bag and started toward the giant. Goliath approached the young man with his shield-bearer in front of him. When he looked around and saw only young David holding a wooden staff, he shouted angrily, "Am I a dog, that you come to me with sticks?" And he cursed David.

Not at all intimidated by this snarling giant, David said to him, "You come to me with a sword, with a spear, and with a javelin. But I come to you in the name of the Lord of hosts, the God of the armies of Israel, whom you have defied. This day the Lord will deliver you into my hand, and I will strike you and take your head from you. And this day I will give

THOUGHT QUESTION:

Why were all the Israelite soldiers afraid of Goliath?

the carcasses of the camp of the Philistines to the birds of the air and the wild beasts of the earth, that all the earth may know that there is a God in Israel. Then all this assembly shall know that the Lord does not save with sword and spear; for the battle is the Lord's, and He will give you into our hands."

In fury, Goliath advanced toward David, towering above the youth. He pushed back his helmet in scorn, and in that moment David was ready to act. He put a stone in his sling and let it fly with all his strength and skill. The stone went straight toward Goliath and buried itself in his forehead!

David the Giant Slayer

Knocked out by the blow, the giant fell forward on his face. David was not carrying a sword, so he raced over to Goliath and grabbed the giant's own sword. He killed Goliath and cut off his head.

When the Philistines saw their champion lying dead on the battlefield, they panicked and ran away in terror, leaving their tents and equipment behind. The armies of Israel rose up with a great shout and pursued the enemy and defeated them. David became the hero of his people.

Chapter 11

ELISHA, PERFORMER OF WONDERS

2 Kings 2:15–4:44; 6:1–7

Elisha was a faithful prophet of God. He had served the prophet Elijah, and when Elijah was taken to heaven, Elisha continued to guide the nation of Israel. The people saw that the Lord was with Elisha, just as He had been with Elijah. They said among themselves, "The spirit of Elijah rests on Elisha."

Elisha was a man of good deeds. He was always helping people. Before he left Jericho, the men of the city asked his advice on a practical matter. The spring of water that supplied the people's needs was bitter. How could the water be made fit to drink? Elisha simply took salt water and poured it into the spring, and the waters became pure and sweet.

The prophet hiked northward on the road to Bethel. While he was passing a town, a crowd of young people came out and mocked him. "Go up, you baldhead! Go up, you baldhead!" they yelled.

Suddenly two female bears came out of the nearby woods and mauled forty-two of these youths. By dishonoring the prophet Elisha, these young people were sinning against God.

One day when Elisha was home at the school of the prophets, a widow came to him with a problem. Her husband had died owing a man money.

Now the man was demanding payment and threatening to take her two sons as slaves to pay the debt.

"Tell me," Elisha asked, "what do you have in the house?"

"Your maidservant has nothing in the house but a jar of oil," she answered.

"Go," he said, "borrow vessels from everywhere, from all your neighbors—empty vessels; do

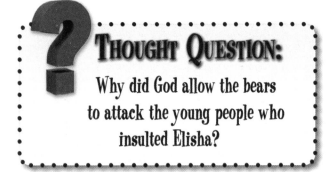

THOUGHT QUESTION:

Why did God allow the bears to attack the young people who insulted Elisha?

not gather just a few. And when you have come in, you shall shut the door behind you and your sons; then pour it into all those vessels, and set aside the full ones."

The woman followed Elisha's instructions and borrowed many empty pots. After closing her front door, she began to pour oil from her jar into the vessels, while her sons kept bringing more pots and jars to her. Her little jar of oil kept pouring and pouring and pouring—and filling pot after pot! When all the pots around her were full, she said to one of her sons, "Bring me another vessel."

"There is not another vessel," he replied. The widow looked in her small jar and saw that it was empty now. She hurried back to Elisha and told him that she had filled a lot of pots with the oil from her one little jar.

"Go, sell the oil and pay your debt," he said, "and you and your sons live on the rest."

Some time later the good prophet was walking through Shunem, a village in the hills north of Mount Carmel. As Elisha walked down the street, a woman saw him and invited him to her home for some food. The prophet passed through Shunem quite often, and after this he always stopped at the home of this woman and her husband for a meal.

One day the woman said to her husband, "Look now, I know that this is a holy man of God, who passes by us regularly. Please, let us make a small upper room on the wall; and let us put a bed for him there, and a table and a chair and a lampstand; so it will be, whenever he comes to us, he can turn in there." Elisha appreciated the family's kindness in giving him a guest room, and he used it whenever he was in Shunem.

Elisha noticed that the woman had no children, and her husband was quite old. Elisha told the woman that God would bless her home with a son. She did not believe the prediction, but a year later, at the time Elisha had said, a baby boy was born.

Several years passed, and the boy grew up. One day he went out into the field where the reapers were harvesting grain. The sun's rays were hot, and the boy's head began to hurt. After a while he went to his father and cried, "My head, my head!"

The father realized that his son had sunstroke. He called a servant and said, "Carry him to his mother." The woman held the boy on her lap until noon, and then he died.

The grief-stricken mother saddled a donkey and hurried to Mount Carmel to find Elisha. She told the prophet what had happened to her only son. Elisha sent his servant Gehazi ahead of him to restore the child's life. When he came to the house, Gehazi placed Elisha's staff on the dead boy's face, as his master had instructed; but there was no sound or response from the child. He returned to Elisha with the bad news.

A short time later, Elisha arrived at the house with the woman from Shunem. He went to the upstairs room where the dead child was lying.

Closing the door, he prayed to God. Then he lay down over the boy, placed his face against the child's face, and put his hands on the boy's hands. The child's skin grew warm, but he did not move. Elisha paced back and forth and prayed again. He stretched himself out on the boy once more, and suddenly the boy sneezed seven times and opened his eyes!

Elisha's servant led the mother up to the room, and when she saw her son alive and well, she bowed at the prophet's feet. "Take up your son," Elisha said. She picked up her son and went out.

Another time, Elisha went to visit the school of the prophets at Gilgal. A bad year of crops had brought famine, and food was scarce. Gehazi began to prepare a pot of stew for the students, and one of the young men went to the field to pick herbs. The student found some wild gourds he had never seen before. He brought them back with the herbs and sliced them into the stew pot. When the men sat down to eat, they noticed a strange taste in the food. "O man of God, there is death in the pot," they said, and they couldn't eat it. The gourds were poisonous.

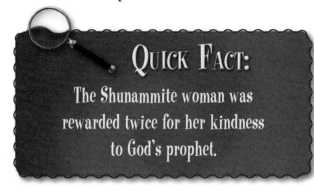

QUICK FACT:

The Shunammite woman was rewarded twice for her kindness to God's prophet.

Elisha said, "Bring some flour," and after throwing a handful into the stew he said, "Serve it to the people that they may eat." The pot of stew had no more poison or sour taste in it.

One day a man brought his tithe—twenty loaves of barley bread and some fresh grain—to Elisha in a knapsack. The prophet thought at once of his hungry students. He told his servant to give it to the people of the school.

The servant asked, "What? Shall I set this before one hundred men?"

Although it seemed that twenty loaves of bread would not go far among so many men, Elisha said, "Give it to the people, that they may eat; for thus says the Lord: 'They shall eat and have some left over.' " God blessed the food, all of the people had plenty to eat, and there was some left over. Elisha always believed that God would care for His people if they trusted in Him.

The sons of the prophets told Elisha that the school did not have enough room for all the students. They decided to go to the bank of the Jordan

River and cut down trees for lumber to build another schoolhouse. Elisha went along with the men. While they were chopping down the trees, the iron head of one student's ax flew off and fell into the river.

"Alas, master! For it was borrowed," the young man said.

"Where did it fall?" asked the man of God.

The student showed Elisha the place where the ax head had fallen into the water. The prophet cut off a stick and threw it in the water. The iron ax head floated to the surface!

GOD SAYS:

"And he showed him the place. So [Elisha] cut off a stick, and threw it in there; and he made the iron float."
–2 Kings 6:6

"Pick it up for yourself," Elisha said. The young man reached out and took the ax head from the surface of the water.

Elisha relied on God for help in every situation, large or small, and he was never disappointed. Trust in God, and He will help you in the same way. There's no doubt about it!

Chapter 12

A Brave Girl Saves a Leper

2 Kings 5

Aram, the country directly north of Israel, had made war against Israel since the days of King Ahab. During the time of Elisha the prophet, the Arameans raided Israel and captured some people who lived near the city of Samaria. Among the prisoners taken to their capital city of Damascus was a girl who had seen the prophet and heard about the wonderful deeds he had done in the name of the true God.

The girl became a maid to the wife of Naaman, commander of the Aramean army. Naaman was a great man and highly respected by his king, because he had led the Aramean army to victory over the Israelites. But he was not happy, because he had a disease called leprosy. In those days there was no cure for leprosy. After some years, the leper would develop a skin rash and likely lose fingers and toes because of injury or infection, and his nose might collapse. Lepers would go blind and eventually die.

The captive Israelite maid loved Naaman's wife, and she was sad because her master had this incurable disease. One day she said to her mistress,

Quick Fact:
Far from her home, the little slave girl was a great witness for God.

67

REAL HEROES

"If only my master were with the prophet who is in Samaria!
For he would heal him of his leprosy."
When Naaman heard these words,
he felt some hope. He decided to

ask his master the king of Aram for permission to go to Israel in search of a cure.

"Go now," the king said, "and I will send a letter to the king of Israel." Naaman set out with chariots, horsemen, and soldiers, and he also carried ten talents of silver, six thousand shekels of gold, and ten beautiful robes as gifts for anyone who could rid him of the dread disease.

Naaman thought that the king of Israel would be able to help him. He arrived in Samaria and presented the letter from the Aramean king to the ruler of Israel. The letter read as follows: "Now be advised, when this letter comes to you, that I have sent Naaman my servant to you, that you may heal him of his leprosy."

After the Israelite king read the letter, he threw it on the floor, tore his robes, and shouted, "Am I God, to kill and make alive, that this man sends a man to me to heal him of his leprosy? Therefore please consider, and see how he seeks a quarrel with me."

Elisha heard how the king of Israel had given the Syrian commander no hope of healing, and he sent a message to the king. "Why have you torn your clothes? Please let him come to me, and he shall know that there is a prophet in Israel."

So Naaman and his men rode in their chariots to the house of Elisha. The prophet did not come out to see the officer from a foreign land. Instead, he sent Gehazi, his servant, who told him, "Go and wash in the Jordan seven times, and your flesh shall be restored to you, and you shall be clean."

The Syrian commander became furious. He said, "Indeed, I said to myself, 'He will surely come out to me, and stand and call on the name of the

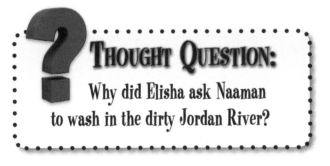

THOUGHT QUESTION:
Why did Elisha ask Naaman to wash in the dirty Jordan River?

Lord his God, and wave his hand over the place, and heal the leprosy.' Are not the Abanah and the Pharpar, the rivers of Damascus, better than all the waters of Israel? Could I not wash in them and be clean?"

Naaman rode away from Elisha's house in a rage. When he had calmed down, one of his servants said to him, "My father, if the prophet had told you to do something great, would you not have done it? How much more then, when he says to you, 'Wash, and be clean'?"

The commander paused to think about these words. He was going to die of leprosy unless he could be healed. Why should he not follow the prophet's simple instructions?

Driving eastward until he came to the Jordan River, Naaman got down from his chariot, took off his robe, and plunged into the water. He dipped himself seven times, as Elisha had commanded. When he went down into the water, there were ugly white patches of skin and raw sores on his body.

GOD SAYS:

"[He] stood before him; and said, 'Indeed, now I know that there is no God in all the earth, except in Israel.' " –2 Kings 5:15

But when he rose up from the water the seventh time, Naaman's skin was like the skin of a child. He was cured of his leprosy!

Jumping in his chariot, Naaman drove back to Elisha's house, his aides following behind. He hurried into the house and stood before the prophet.

"Indeed, now I know that there is no God in all the earth, except in Israel," said Naaman. "Now therefore, please take a gift from your servant."

"As the Lord lives, before whom I stand, I will receive nothing," said Elisha.

Although Naaman urged the prophet to accept his rich presents, he would not take anything. The commander went on his way northward toward home.

Gehazi, Elisha's servant, had listened to all the talk about silver and gold and beautiful robes. His own clothing was shabby and patched. After Naaman had been gone a short while, Gehazi hurried after him. When the Syrian officer saw the man running along the road, he stopped his chariots and went back to meet Elisha's servant. "Is all well?" he asked.

"All is well," said Gehazi. "My master has sent me, saying, 'Indeed, just now two young men of the sons of the prophets have come to me from the mountains of Ephraim. Please give them a talent of silver and two changes of garments.' "

Of course, Gehazi was lying. But Naaman was so happy to be healed of his leprosy that he gave the servant more than he had asked for. "Please, take two talents," said Naaman, heaping the treasure and clothes upon the man.

Gehazi returned to his house and hid the gifts. Then he went and stood before Elisha. The prophet said, "Where did you go, Gehazi?"

"Your servant did not go anywhere," Gehazi lied.

"Did not my heart go with you when the man turned back from his chariot to meet you?" said the prophet. "Is it time to receive money and to receive clothing, olive groves and vineyards, sheep and oxen, male and female servants? Therefore the leprosy of Naaman shall cling to you and your descendants forever."

So Gehazi left Elisha's presence a leper as white as snow.

It must have been a day of excitement and happiness when Naaman arrived home. His wife marveled when she saw that her husband was free from the fearful disease. The captive maid must have been overjoyed for her master! Not only had he returned well and strong, but now he worshiped the true God whom she loved. Because this faithful girl had been true to her God in a foreign country, her prayers were answered.

Chapter 13

JONAH'S NARROW ESCAPE

The Book of Jonah

Far to the east of Israel and Syria arose the great empire of Assyria. Its kings were mighty rulers in their capital city of Ninevah. When they sent out their armies, they conquered the smaller nations. By this time, the Israelites had divided into two separate nations—Israel and Judah—each with its own king. When the king of Israel heard about the Assyrians, he was afraid, and rightly so. The day would come when the fierce warriors from Nineveh would attack his capital city of Samaria.

In the little country of Judah, the land of the two tribes of Benjamin and Judah, lived a prophet named Jonah. The Lord sent a message to him. "Arise, go to Nineveh, that great city, and cry out against it; for their wickedness has come up before Me."

The prophet might have been afraid to face the people of Ninevah, or he might not have wanted to take a long trip to a foreign country. Whatever his reason, Jonah hurried in the opposite direction. He went west to Joppa by the sea, instead of heading east for Nineveh. When Jonah arrived at the seaport, he bought a ticket on a ship sailing to Tarshish, a city far to the west. *Now,* thought Jonah, *I will get away where God cannot find me.*

After the ship had sailed from the harbor to the open sea, the prophet went down into the hold and fell asleep. Soon a terrible wind storm struck the boat. The wind howled, and huge waves crashed over the sides of the vessel. Even the sailors were frightened, and each man called on his pagan gods for help. The storm grew so severe that it seemed the ship would be swamped. In desperation the crew threw the cargo overboard to lighten the ship.

The captain went down into the hold of the ship and found Jonah sound asleep. "What do you mean, sleeper?" asked the captain. "Arise, call on your God; perhaps your God will consider us, so that we may not perish."

The men on board said one to another, "Come, let us cast lots, that we may know for whose cause this trouble has come upon us."

So they cast lots, which is like throwing dice, and the lot fell on Jonah. They looked at this man who had bought passage on the ship, and they said, "Please tell us! For whose cause is this trouble upon us? What is your occupation? And where do you come from? What is your country? And of what people are you?"

Jonah told the men that he was a Hebrew and that he had run away from his God-given assignment. He told them that he worshiped the Creator of the sea and the land. When the men heard this, they were terrified and asked, "Why have you done this?"

After talking together, the sailors asked Jonah, "What shall we do to you that the sea may be calm for us?" The storm was getting worse by the minute.

"Pick me up," said Jonah, "and throw me into the sea; then the sea will become calm for you. For I know that this great tempest is because of me."

The sailors refused to throw Jonah overboard. They put out the oars and tried to row the ship back toward land. But the heavy waves beat against the ship, and the storm grew worse. Finally they cried out to the God of heaven in their terror, saying, "We pray, O Lord,

GOD SAYS:
"Now the Lord had prepared a great fish to swallow Jonah." –Jonah 1:17

please do not let us perish for this man's life, and do not charge us with innocent blood; for You, O Lord, have done as it pleased You."

So they picked up Jonah and tossed him overboard into the roaring sea. When they had done this, the storm died down and the waves grew calm.

Jonah was trying to keep his head above the waves when "a great fish" came swimming toward him. He must have cried out in fear and terror as a fish opened its huge mouth. The next thing Jonah knew, he felt himself being sucked into the giant jaws and swallowed! Down, down he went into the belly of the fish. "The Lord had prepared a great fish to swallow Jonah," the Bible says.

For three days and three nights Jonah tossed about in the stomach of the great fish. He must have been panicked and frightened. He knew what was happening, however, and he prayed to God, promising that if he was saved alive he would obey and go to Nineveh to preach.

After three days the fish threw up Jonah on the beach, and the prophet returned to his home, thankful that his life had been spared. Soon the message of the Lord came to Jonah a second time, saying, "Arise, go to Nineveh, that great city, and preach to it the message that I tell you."

This time Jonah did not hesitate. He started for Nineveh immediately. When he reached the great city on the banks of the Tigris River he went through the streets shouting, "Yet forty days, and Nineveh shall be overthrown!"

The people of Nineveh were sinful and wicked, but when they heard this warning they began to mourn. The king sent out a decree that every person should fast and repent of his sins and call upon God. Very quickly the whole city turned away from evil ways. When the Lord saw that the Assyrians wanted to do right, He determined not to destroy Nineveh.

But when Jonah found out that the city would not be destroyed, he was angry. It seemed to him that his work had been for nothing. He decided that life wasn't worth living, and he prayed, "Therefore now, O Lord, please take my life from me, for it is better for me to die than to live!"

The Lord said, "Is it right for you to be angry?"

Without answering the question, Jonah left the city and walked to a hillside where he could look over the big metropolis. He built a shelter for shade because the sun was very warm. The Lord God made a wild gourd vine grow over the shelter to relieve the misery of the angry prophet. Jonah was thankful for the cool shade of the vine.

> **QUICK FACT:**
> Nineveh was the capital of Assyria—a nation known for its cruelty.

The prophet stayed in his shelter all night. The next morning, God allowed a worm to eat through the vine so that it quickly withered. Then a hot wind blew, and the sun beat down on Jonah. Again he wished he were dead.

The Lord said, "You have had pity on the plant for which you have not labored, nor made it grow, which came up in a night and perished in a night. And should I not pity Nineveh, that

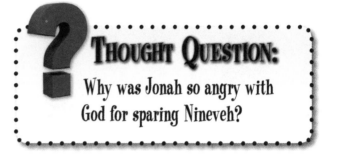

THOUGHT QUESTION:
Why was Jonah so angry with God for sparing Nineveh?

great city, in which are more than one hundred and twenty thousand persons who cannot discern between their right hand and their left—and much livestock?"

In this way God taught the prophet from Judah that He loves people of all nations and all races. It was a wonderful example of the Father's mercy. God is ready to forgive all who will repent of their sins, if they will turn to Him with all their heart and mind. Jonah learned, too, that he could never run away from the Lord who sees all that we do and who hears all that we say.

Chapter 14

A FIERY FURNACE

Daniel 3; 4

God had given King Nebuchadnezzar of Babylon a dream about a large image made of different metals. Its head was gold, representing Nebuchadnezzar's kingdom of Babylon. But the king wasn't satisfied. He didn't want Babylon to be just the head of gold; he wanted his empire to last forever. He wasn't willing to accept the meaning of the dream God had given him—that other kingdoms would arise after Babylon had passed off the scene of action. To demonstrate the power and everlasting nature of his kingdom he ordered workmen to make a giant statue more than a hundred feet tall—and to cover the whole statue with gold. He had the statue set up on the plain of Dura.

Then Nebuchadnezzar sent for all his governors, judges, counselors, and other high officials to come from all the provinces of the kingdom for the dedication of the golden statue. On the day set for the celebration, a vast multitude of people assembled on the plain of Dura.

A herald shouted King Nebuchadnezzar's instructions to the crowd, "To you it is commanded, O peoples, nations, and languages, that at the time you hear the sound of the horn, flute, harp, lyre, and psaltery, in symphony with all kinds of music, you shall fall down and worship the gold image that

A Fiery Furnace

King Nebuchadnezzar has set up; and whoever does not fall down and worship shall be cast immediately into the midst of a burning fiery furnace."

As soon as the music began to play, all the people bowed before the golden statue, as the king had commanded.

All the people except three! Shadrach, Meshach, and Abednego, who along with Daniel had been taken as captives to Babylon from Judah. These young men had remained faithful to God in Babylon and had risen to be given positions of influence in the kingdom. Now they stood tall, refusing to worship the statue. They would worship only God. No doubt Daniel would have stayed standing with them, but he was evidently not at the celebration.

As soon as certain Babylonians saw the three Hebrews still standing, they hurried to Nebuchadnezzar and said, "O king, live forever! . . . There are certain Jews whom you have set over the affairs of the province of Babylon: Shadrach, Meshach, and Abed-Nego; these men, O king, have not paid due regard to you. They do not serve your gods or worship the gold image which you have set up."

The king commanded that the three Hebrews be brought to him, and with fury in his eyes he said, "Is it true, Shadrach, Meshach, and Abed-Nego, that you do not serve my gods or worship the gold image which I have set up?" Nebuchadnezzar said that he would give them another chance. But if they did not bow down as he had commanded, he would have them thrown into the furnace of fire.

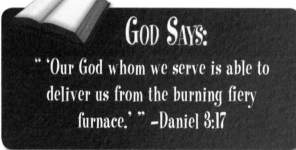

GOD SAYS:
" 'Our God whom we serve is able to deliver us from the burning fiery furnace.' " –Daniel 3:17

"O Nebuchadnezzar, we have no need to answer you in this matter," the young officials said. "Our God whom we serve is able to deliver us from the burning fiery furnace, and He will deliver us from your hand, O king. But if not, let it be known to you, O king, that we do not serve your gods, nor will we worship the gold image which you have set up."

When Nebuchadnezzar heard this straightforward reply, he was filled with rage against the three princes who refused to bow at his command. He ordered the furnace to be heated seven times hotter than usual. Then he commanded some of his strongest soldiers to bind the three young men and throw them into the super-heated furnace. The three Hebrews fell down in the middle of the fire. The furnace was so hot that the soldiers who threw the men into the fire were killed by the terrible heat.

King Nebuchadnezzar watched for a moment, and then he became alarmed. He called his ministers and asked, "Did we not cast three men bound into the midst of the fire?"

"True, O king," they answered.

"Look!" he said, "I see four men loose, walking in the midst of the fire; and they are not hurt, and the form of the fourth is like the Son of God."

Then King Nebuchadnezzar edged close to the furnace and called out, "Shadrach, Meshach, and Abed-Nego, servants of the Most High God, come out, and come here."

The three men walked out of the furnace, and the amazed officials and the king gathered around. They saw that the fire had not burned them or even singed their hair. There was not even the smell of fire on their clothing!

Now King Nebuchadnezzar was ready to give the God of heaven praise for protecting the three young men. "Blessed be the God of Shadrach, Meshach, and Abed-Nego, who sent His Angel and delivered His servants who trusted in Him, and they have frustrated the king's word, and yielded their bodies, that they should not serve nor worship any god except their own God!" He made a decree that anyone in the entire kingdom who said anything bad about the God of these three men would be executed and their home destroyed.

QUICK FACT:

When Nebuchadnezzar realized the young men weren't hurt, he praised them for their courage and their God.

Then the king promoted Shadrach, Meshach, and Abednego and gave them more responsibility in the kingdom.

Nebuchadnezzar was so impressed by the power of God in caring for His people that he sent a message to all the people of his kingdom. It said,

> Peace be multiplied to you.
> I thought it good to declare the signs and wonders that the Most
>   High God has worked for me.
> How great are His signs,
> And how mighty His wonders!
> His kingdom is an everlasting kingdom,
> And His dominion is from generation to generation.

Unfortunately, King Nebuchadnezzar didn't continue to remember God and His power. Daniel tried to point the king in the right direction. He pleaded with Nebuchadnezzar, "O king, let my advice be acceptable to you; break off your sins by being righteous, and your iniquities by showing mercy to the poor. Perhaps there may be a lengthening of your prosperity."

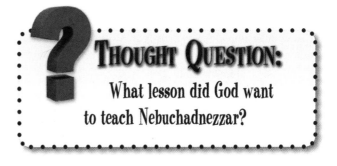

THOUGHT QUESTION:
What lesson did God want to teach Nebuchadnezzar?

But Nebuchadnezzar soon went back to his old proud ways. One day as he was walking around his palace surveying Babylon, a great city of many wonders, he said out loud, "Is not this great Babylon, that I have built for a royal dwelling by my mighty power and for the honor of my majesty?"

He took all the credit for God's blessings to himself. He forgot how God had worked a miracle to protect Shadrach, Meshach, and Abednego when he had thrown them into the fiery furnace. He forgot how they had come out of the fierce fire without being burned at all or even smelling like smoke!

Chapter 15

DANIEL IN THE DEN OF LIONS

Daniel 5; 6

King Nebuchadnezzar died, but the kingdom of Babylon continued in power and greatness. Belshazzar, Nebuchadnezzar's grandson, was placed in authority in the capital city. This weak man was foolish; he loved only pleasure and glory. Soon his nation faced grave danger. The armies of the Medes and the Persians attacked Babylon.

Belshazzar did not worry about the enemy. He thought the strong walls of the city would make it impossible for any enemy to enter. He made a great feast and invited a thousand lords and nobles to attend. Princes and statesmen came and drank wine and praised their gods of silver and gold.

During the feast, the fingers of a man's hand appeared and began to write on the wall by a lamp stand. A hush fell over the royal banquet hall. The king turned pale, and his knees knocked together. He shouted for his astrologers and fortune tellers to come. "Whoever reads this writing, and tells me its interpretation," the king said to them, "shall be clothed with purple and have a chain of gold around his neck; and he shall be the third ruler in the kingdom."

None of the wise men who entered the banquet hall and saw the writing on the wall could read it. The queen mother heard about what was happen-

ing at the feast of Belshazzar and his lords, and she came into the hall. She remembered that Daniel had interpreted dreams for King Nebuchadnezzar many years before. "Let Daniel be called," she advised her son, "and he will give the interpretation."

Daniel was hurriedly brought in before the king. When Belshazzar saw the aging prophet he said, "Are you that Daniel who is one of the captives from Judah, whom my father the king brought from Judah? I have heard of you, that the Spirit of God is in you, and that light and understanding and excellent wisdom are found in you. Now the wise men, the astrologers, have been brought in before me, that they should read this writing and make known to me its interpretation, but they could not give the interpretation of the thing. . . . Now if you can read the writing and make known to me its interpretation, you shall be clothed with purple and have a chain of gold around your neck, and shall be the third ruler in the kingdom."

"Let your gifts be for yourself, and give your rewards to another," Daniel said bluntly. "Yet I will read the writing to the king, and make known to him the interpretation."

Daniel then reminded Belshazzar of Nebuchadnezzar's mistake in forgetting God and the terrible punishment that came on him. "But you his son, Belshazzar, have not humbled your heart, although you knew all this. And you have lifted yourself up against the Lord of heaven."

Turning to the writing on the wall, Daniel translated the words. "MENE: God has numbered your kingdom, and finished it; TEKEL: You have been weighed in the balances, and found wanting; PERES: Your kingdom has been divided, and given to the Medes and Persians."

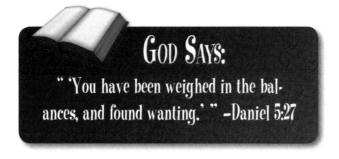

GOD SAYS:
" 'You have been weighed in the balances, and found wanting.' " –Daniel 5:27

True to his word, Belshazzar had Daniel clothed in purple, a gold chain placed around his neck, and he was proclaimed third ruler in the kingdom. But that very night the army of the Medes and Persians entered the city, overcame the guards, and killed Belshazzar, king of Babylon.

Darius the Mede became king and took over the empire. Daniel continued to serve in the court under the new king. In fact, King Darius made Daniel one of the three chiefs of his 120 governors. Daniel distinguished himself as honest and wise, so the king considered setting him over the whole kingdom. Of course, some of the other officials were jealous of Daniel, and they plotted how they might get him into trouble. But try as they might, they could find no fault with him. The jealous plotters discussed among themselves and concluded, "We shall not find any charge against this Daniel unless we find it against him concerning the law of his God."

QUICK FACT:
It was Daniel's good character that made his enemies jealous of him.

They thought and thought and at last came up with an evil plan. The officials hurried to the king and said, "King Darius, live forever! All the governors of the kingdom, the administrators and satraps, the counselors and advisors, have consulted together to establish a royal statute and to make a firm decree, that whoever petitions any god or man for thirty days, except you, O king, shall be cast into the den of lions. Now, O king, establish the decree and sign the writing, so that it cannot be changed, according to the law of the Medes and Persians, which does not alter."

These men knew that Daniel prayed only to the God of heaven. They did not mention this to the king, however. They knew that if King Darius realized how the law would endanger Daniel's life, he would not sign the decree. King Darius was pleased with the decree and signed it, not suspecting what was behind it.

When Daniel, the prophet of God, heard about the decree, he went to his house. Every day, three times a day, Daniel opened his windows toward Jerusalem. Then he would kneel and give thanks to the Lord. On this day Daniel prayed as he always had.

His enemies rushed to the house and found Daniel in the act of praying to God. They hurried back to the palace and came before the king.

"Have you not signed a decree," they asked, trying to act natural, "that every man who petitions any god or man within thirty days, except you, O king, shall be cast into the den of lions?"

"The thing is true, according to the law of the Medes and Persians, which does not alter," the king said.

"Daniel, who is one of the captives from Judah, does not show due regard for you, O king, or for the decree that you have signed, but makes his petition three times a day."

When King Darius heard this, he was extremely upset with himself. Immediately he set his heart on saving Daniel. All day the king worked to find a solution and deliver his faithful governor. At sunset the crafty officials approached King Darius and said, "Know, O king, that it is the law of the Medes and Persians that no decree or statute which the king establishes may be changed."

The king gave the order, and Daniel was thrown into the underground den of lions. King Darius came out to the den and called down to Daniel, "Your God, whom you serve continually, He will deliver you." Then the entrance of the den was covered with a large stone. The king sealed it in wax with his signet ring.

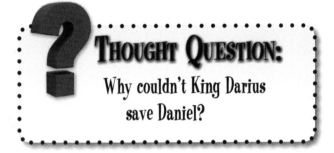

THOUGHT QUESTION:

Why couldn't King Darius save Daniel?

That night the king did not eat. He could not sleep. His thoughts were on Daniel in the den of snarling lions. In the morning, as soon as it was light, King Darius hurried to the den and called in a sad voice, "Daniel, servant of the living God, has your God, whom you serve continually, been able to deliver you from the lions?"

The king listened.

"O king, live forever!" Daniel said. "My God sent His angel and shut the lions' mouths, so that they have not hurt me, because I was found innocent before Him; and also, O king, I have done no wrong before you."

The king was exceedingly happy. He gave orders for his friend to be taken up from the lions' den. Soon Daniel was standing on the ground again, and he had no injuries at all, not even a scratch!

Darius then commanded that all the men who had accused Daniel should be brought to the lions' den. The wicked officials, with their wives and children, were thrown down to the lions. These lions were ferocious, and they broke the bones of the people before they even hit the bottom of the den.

Then Darius wrote this decree to all nations:

"Peace be multiplied to you.

"I make a decree that in every dominion of my kingdom men must tremble and fear before the God of Daniel."

Daniel the aging prophet continued to prosper during the reign of Darius, and he was loyal to God all the days of his life.

Chapter 16

ESTHER, QUEEN OF GREAT COURAGE

The Book of Esther

When Xerxes became the ruler of the Medo-Persian Empire he decided to choose a new queen from among the beautiful maidens of the empire. Esther, a Jewish girl, was chosen to be the new queen, although Xerxes didn't know that she was a Jew. Neither did anyone else at the royal court.

Mordecai, Esther's cousin, was a minor government official. One day he overheard two angry servants plotting to kill the king. He reported the plot and the details of the incident were written down in the official records.

About this time, Haman, a proud prince of the court, was promoted to be above all the other princes. The king commanded that all the officials and servants should bow to him. But Mordecai did not bow to Haman, because he had been taught to worship God alone. Haman was filled with rage. What could he do? Soon Haman decided on an evil plan. He would do more than punish Mordecai alone. He would punish all the Jews in the kingdom. Of course, he didn't know that Queen Esther was a Jew.

Haman approached King Xerxes

QUICK FACT:
The Persians worshiped their gods through their rulers, which is why Mordecai wouldn't bow down to Haman.

and said, "There is a certain people scattered and dispersed among the people in all the provinces of your kingdom; their laws are different from all other people's, and they do not keep the king's laws. Therefore it is not fitting for the king to let them remain. If it pleases the king, let a decree be written that they be destroyed."

Since the king did not know Haman's real purpose, he agreed. Of course, he still did not know that his beautiful queen was a Jew.

When Mordecai heard about the decree, he tore his clothes and mourned deeply. He knew that this law doomed his people to destruction. As the decree reached Jews living in different parts of the empire, they began to weep. Many of them put on sackcloth and ashes and fasted and prayed.

Mordecai sent a message to Queen Esther saying that she must go to the king and beg for the lives of her people.

Esther sent her servant to remind Mordecai that anyone who approached the king without being summoned would be put to death unless the king held out his golden scepter to that person and pardoned him. How could Esther approach the king and plead for her people? She hadn't seen the king for the last thirty days.

Trusting in the Lord to help his people, Mordecai sent word back to the queen, "Do not think in your heart that you will escape in the king's palace any more than all the other Jews. For if you remain completely silent at this time, relief and deliverance will arise for the

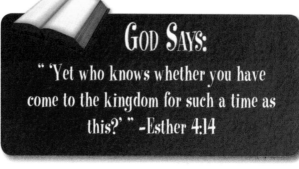

GOD SAYS:

" 'Yet who knows whether you have come to the kingdom for such a time as this?' " -Esther 4:14

Jews from another place, but you and your father's house will perish. Yet who knows whether you have come to the kingdom for such a time as this?"

When Esther received this challenge, she sent word to her cousin: "I will go to the king, which is against the law; and if I perish, I perish!"

Esther put on her royal robes and went to the inner courtyard of the king's house. King Xerxes, seated on his throne, saw the queen standing outside. He held out his golden scepter, and Esther came near and touched it.

"What do you wish, Queen Esther?" asked the king. "What is your request? It shall be given to you—up to half the kingdom!"

"If it pleases the king, let the king and Haman come today to the banquet that I have prepared for him."

So the king and Haman went to the banquet that Esther had prepared. There, King Xerxes asked her again what she really wanted. Esther invited the king and Haman to dinner the following day—when she would reveal her request.

Haman happily rushed home to tell his wife that he was again to be the special guest of the queen. "Yet all this avails me nothing, so long as I see Mordecai the Jew sitting at the king's gate," he finished with a frown.

Haman's wife suggested that he build a tall gallows and that the next morning he ask the king for permission to hang Mordecai on it. Haman liked the idea and had the gallows erected at once.

That night the king could not sleep. To help him pass the hours he had a scribe bring the records of the kingdom and read them to him. Soon the scribe came to the account of how Mordecai had caught two traitors who had planned to kill the king.

"What honor or dignity has been bestowed on Mordecai for this?" Xerxes asked.

The servants waiting on the king said, "Nothing has been done for him."

By this time it was early morning. The king said, "Who is in the court?"

Now Haman had gotten up very early and come to the palace to request that the king hang Mordecai. One of the king's servants noticed him and announced, "Haman is there, standing in the court."

"Let him come in," said the king.

So Haman approached, and the king asked him, "What shall be done for the man whom the king delights to honor?"

Haman thought to himself, *Whom would the king delight to honor more than me?* So the proud man said, "For the man whom the king delights to honor, let a royal robe be brought which the king has worn, and a horse on which the king has ridden, which has a royal crest placed on its head. Then let this robe and horse be delivered

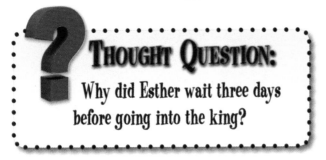

THOUGHT QUESTION:

Why did Esther wait three days before going into the king?

to the hand of one of the king's most noble princes, that he may array the man whom the king delights to honor. Then parade him on horseback through the city square, and proclaim before him: 'Thus shall it be done to the man whom the king delights to honor!' "

The king said to Haman, "Hurry, take the robe and the horse, as you have suggested, and do so for Mordecai the Jew who sits within the king's gate! Leave nothing undone of all that you have spoken."

Knowing that he would be executed if he didn't obey, Haman took the robe and the horse, put the robe on Mordecai, and led him on horseback through the city square, shouting, "Thus shall it be done to the man whom the king delights to honor!"

Afterward, Haman rushed home weeping and with his head covered. Soon the king's servants arrived to take Haman to Queen Esther's second ban-

QUICK FACT:
In Persia, once the king made a law, it could not be changed.

quet. As the king and Haman dined with her, King Xerxes asked again, "What is your petition, Queen Esther? It shall be granted you. And what is your request, up to half the kingdom? It shall be done!"

"If I have found favor in your sight, O king," Esther answered, "and if it pleases the king, let my life be given me at my petition, and my people at my request. For we have been sold, my people and I, to be destroyed, to be killed, and to be annihilated."

"Who is he, and where is he, who would dare presume in his heart to do such a thing?" demanded the king.

"The adversary and enemy is this wicked Haman!" said Esther, pointing to the chief prince.

King Xerxes stood up in great anger and went out into the palace garden. Haman was terrified. He stood before Queen Esther and begged for his life. When the king came back to the banquet room, Haman had fallen across the couch where Esther was sitting. The king said, "Will he also assault the queen while I am in the house?"

As he said this, his servants covered Haman's face. They knew that he was already condemned to death. One of the eunuchs said to the king, "Look!

The gallows, fifty cubits high, which Haman made for Mordecai, who spoke good on the king's behalf, is standing at the house of Haman."

The king said, "Hang him on it!"

So Haman was hanged on his own gallows.

Then King Xerxes called a scribe to write a message for the Jews in all the provinces of the kingdom, telling them they could gather in groups and fight for their lives on the day that had been set for their destruction. The Jews gathered in armed bands and defended themselves and their families on that day. The following day the Jews celebrated and held feasts. And Queen Esther issued a proclamation that the Jews should keep that day annually as a day of feasting and joy.